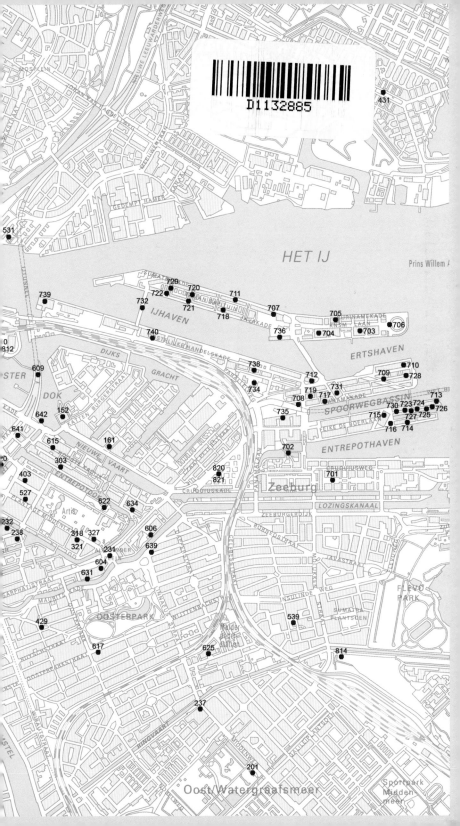

Amsterdam Architecture

A Guide

Edited by Guus Kemme & Gaston Bekkers

Photographs by Jan Derwig

Paul Broers
Marlies Buurman
Judikje Kiers
Marga van Klinken
Wilfred van Leeuwen
Birgitte de Maar
Erik Mattie
Renate Meijer
Tim Verlaan
Jouke van der Werf

Sixth expanded and revised edition

THOTH Publishers Bussum

© 2010 Gaston Bekkers and THOTH Publishers, Nieuwe 's-Gravelandseweg 3,
1405 HH Bussum, The Netherlands
WWW.THOTH.NL
© 2010 Photographs Jan Derwig bfn and THOTH Publishers

Translation: Chris Gordon, Marja Kramp, Don Mader (Words & Pictures,
Rotterdam), Lodewijk Odé and Paul Willcox
Design: Opera Ontwerpers, Breda
Printing and binding: Conti Tipocolor (Italy)

ISBN 978 90 6868 562 6

Contents

Acknowledgements

With the enormous wave of construction over the last decade, the architectural guide to Amsterdam was obviously due for revision. In light of the interest from architecture tourists, the city's expansion with the Eastern Docklands region can be termed a great success. Amsterdam has a new attraction of stature to join its ring canals, since 2010 on UNESCO's World Heritage List. But there is also a good deal elsewhere in the city which is well worth making the effort to see.

I would first like to thank Tim Verlaan for his contributions on recent projects in the new chapter 'Latest projects (2005-2010)'. Without his assistance the updating of the architecture guide would not have gone as smoothly as it has. I further want to thank publisher Kees van den Hoek and photographer Jan Derwig for all their help and fine cooperation. And of course I cannot forget my debt of gratitude to all the authors who have been involved with the guide from the very beginning.

At the end of 2000, just two days before New Year's, Guus Kemme died much before his time. The guide was his initiative. As a publisher and as the owner of the Architectura & Natura book store he contributed mightily to architecture and landscape design in his short life. Thanks to his enormous enthusiasm we have now been able to realise a sixth edition of the original English publication. I therefore wish you great pleasure in your voyage of discovery through the architectural history of Amsterdam, a unique city.

Gaston Bekkers

Introduction

The great variety in the architecture of Amsterdam has often been a reason for architects, art historians or just lovers of fine buildings to pay a visit to the city. *Amsterdam Architecture* is intended as an introduction and a companion for these visitors. The chronological arrangement of the guide gives a picture of the architecture through the ages. *Amsterdam Architecture* opens with an introduction to the architectural history of the city, which is followed by eight separate periods into which the history is divided. Each period includes an introduction which is followed by a great number of illustrations with the address, the name of the architect and the name and date of each building. Although this guide can only give a limited number of examples, every effort has been made to create a picture which is as representative as possible. Apart from this there is a list of the bodies engaged in architectural history, the preservation of monuments and historic buildings, 'architectural walks', lectures, etc. The guide concludes with an index which contains the names of all the streets included in the guide and the names of the persons and the buildings respectively. The maps on the insides of the cover show the location of the buildings illustrated in the guide. The numbers correspond to the numbers in bold face on the bottom line of the captions. This line also indicates the accessibility of the building to the public (□ = open to the public, ■ = closed to the public). Fore more than one reason the centre of Amsterdam cannot be visited by car. The ring of concentric canals was not built to hold so many cars and the exhaust fumes are harmful to the monuments. Adequate car-parking space can be found outside the city centre and in the suburbs, from which there are good connections to the centre by public transport. It is, therefore, advisable to walk or to cycle (rent-a-bike) within the ring of concentric canals. Public transport to each of the buildings outside this ring is indicated.

The history of a densely populated city

It has been said that Amsterdam is a laboratory for town-planning experiments. The creativity of a people that has to make the most of the space granted to it becomes apparent in the sequence of organic growth and conscious planning. An aerial view of Amsterdam shows how the diversity of the various districts increases towards the perimeter. In the middle lies the famous crescent-shape of the seventeenth century concentric canals around which the ring of nineteenth century areas and, on the outskirts, the many developments of the present century, spreading far into the landscape of Noord-Holland.

Beginnings

Amsterdam is situated on the river IJ, and was built when it was not yet cut off from the Zuiderzee (renamed the IJsselmeer). The river Amstel, together with the Dam, which the inhabitants built in the river around 1270, gave the town its name. A finger of land opposite the mouth of the Amstel protected the port against the westerly winds, while the tidal flow of the Zuiderzee prevented the port from silting up. The reclamation of many of the lakes surrounding the city made the thick, marshy layer of peat available for building. The buildings were all of timber, but fires in 1421 and 1453 made it essential to build in brick. To support this, long wood en piles were driven into the ground and held together by a framework. Dikes protected the land against the threatening seas but, even in the eighteenth century, were not able to prevent the farmlands from being flooded: a spectacle that scared the wits out of many a foreign visitor.

When in 1275, Amsterdam was granted exemption from paying tolls on Dutch waterways; it was able to devote itself to trade as well as to fishing. In the four-teenth and fifteenth centuries, the town became the most important port of call for many ships on their way from the German Hansa towns to Bruges, the most important trading town of the time.

The favourable position of Amsterdam and the development of small, manoeu-vrable ships led to an increase in trade with the Baltic and the town itself became a permanent annual fair, at which grain and other commodities could be stored for long periods. The cargo trade and fishing stimulated industry and attracted many unemployed labourers from the countryside. The first towns-people lived along the banks of the river Amstel in the Warmoesstraat and the Nieuwendijk. A wooden rampart was surrounded by the Nieuwezijds Voorburgwal and the Oudezijds Voorburgwal. In the fifteenth century the town was twice enlarged with new moats without filling up the preceding ones. The oblique dike paths became linking alleys and streets.

In 1425, when the Geldersekade and the Kloveniersburgwal in the east and the Singel in the west were built, the town was provided with its first brick fortress, with gateways, perimeter towers and round bastions. Nevertheless, the new extensions were not sufficient to cope with the increasing stream of immigrants and very soon the town literally burst at the seams. In defiance of the interests of the landowners, the inhabitants of the carpentry workshops to the east of the city, in the area around what is now the Jodenbreestraat (then known as the Lastage), demanded protection. The landowners, who were often also members of the city council, feared a drop in the price of land. In 1589, the inhabitants got what they wanted. The carpentry workshops were removed to the islands to the east of the city and the Lastage became an exclusively residential area.

The seventeenth century concentric canals

Amsterdam, which remained Roman Catholic longer than other Dutch towns, only chose the side of William of Orange during the revolt of the Northern Netherlands against the Spanish Habsburger kings (1568-1648). In 1578 when the Protestants took over the city, Amsterdam gained a reputation for freedom and tolerance. The already substantial influx of refugees grew considerably in 1585 when the powerful city of Antwerp fell into Spanish hands and was cut off from the sea. Experienced Antwerp merchants and many poor Protestants took refuge in Amsterdam and gave impetus to trade. An important contribution was also made by rich Portuguese Jews. Trade was not restricted to the Baltic and the Mediterranean; Dutch ships swarmed over the seven seas. With a fleet larger than the English, French and Spanish put together, Amsterdam became the biggest trading town and depot of the seventeenth century. The expansion of the town stimulated the establishment of whale-oil factories, ship-yards, soap works, textile industry and many other industries and gave rise to financial institutions such as the banks and the stock exchange.

Recruiting cheap labour became more important for the landowning merchants and entrepreneurs than land speculation. Between 1570 and 1640, the population had increased from 30.000 to 139.000. It is clear that the decision of 1609 to undertake a considerable expansion of the city had been absolutely essential. All remaining open spaces were built on and former monasteries were requisitioned for public services. Increasing prosperity resulted in increasing social differences.

Citizens who had become rich wished to live far away from the smell of the docks and the noise of the warehouses. This wish had to be taken into consideration in the new development. The western section of the new expansion, as far as the Leidsegracht, was completed between 1612 and 1625 and the eastern expansion was commenced in 1658. The ramparts, with 26 bastions, were laid out like a barbed chain around the city. Of the old city gates, only the Sint Antoniespoort remained and the old city towers were provided with spires. New gateways appeared on the exit roads to Haarlem, Leiden, Utrecht, Weesp and Muiden.

Within the city walls, the western part was parcelled out in two ways. The well-to-do citizens of the mansions in the Warmoesstraat and the Kalverstraat settled in the first section: Herengracht, Keizersgracht and Prinsengracht. The plots were laid out by Frans Hendriksz. Oetgens and Hendrick Jacobsz. Staets, on a mathematical basis rather than following the existing pattern of drainage ditches and pastures. This approach had already been applied to the Oostelijke Eilanden of Uilenburg, Rapenburg and Marken. However, the straight radial roads connecting the canals provided only poor links to the city centre and the way in which the second area to be parcelled out, known as the Jordaan, was attached, was equally unsatisfactory. In the Jordaan, where small tradesmen and many Jews had settled, the division into lots did follow the existing pattern of ditches and pastures.

In dividing land into lots, space was reserved in both the Jordaan and within the belt of concentric canals for churches and public buildings which were not surrounded by large squares and parks. Neither public gardens nor wide prospects will be found in seventeenth century Amsterdam. The area to the west of the Amstel was quickly built up, whereas the eastern section lagged behind. Many Jewish immigrants settled here and rich Amsterdammers founded many charitable institutions. Between the concentric canals and the Oostelijke Eilanden, the Plantage was built, a promenade park with small country houses for well-to-do citizens. Now the Botanical Gardens are situated here.

The prosperity of Amsterdam was maintained throughout the eighteenth century even though the port was surpassed in importance by London, Hamburg and Bremen. The rate of population growth decreased. The latest developments were sufficient to house all the inhabitants. Wealthy citizens built country houses along the Vecht and in the Watergraafsmeer which had been reclaimed in 1628. Only Frankendael still reminds us of the former affluence.

The nineteenth century: a new start

In 1813 the French troops of Napoleon left the Kingdom of the Netherlands in a state of collapse. With the financial support and economic insight of King William I the Netherlands tried to revive the former glories of Amsterdam. In the first part of the nineteenth century improvements to the infrastructure laid the basis for economic development. This was only to gain momentum in the second part of the nineteenth century. The port was dredged and cut off from the Zuiderzee and reconnected with the sea in the north by the Noord-Hollandsch Kanaal (1825). The opening of the Noordzeekanaal in 1876 and the Merwedekanaal in 1896 enabled Amsterdam to develop into an important port for transferring cargoes. The first railway, to Haarlem, was opened in 1839. Soon afterwards lines were laid to Utrecht (1843) and to Hilversum (1874), from the Weesperpoortstation. Not until 1889, the Centraal Station was built on an artificial island facing the waterfront on the axis of the Damrak to connect the lines from Utrecht to Haarlem.

The improved infrastructure stimulated industry. Shipbuilding flourished in the thirties and several factories were built on the outskirts of the town. The tram system and the gas and electricity companies were in private hands. This suited the more progressive liberals, who after 1865 had a great deal of influence in the city council. The liberal council had to deal with the problems of a city that was very much impoverished, had a great number of unemployed people

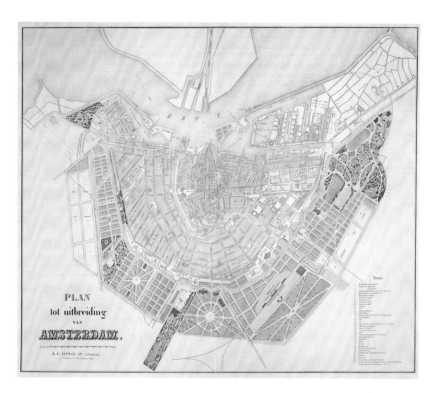

Development Plan
Amsterdam, 1866,
J.G. van Niftrik

and an exodus of well-to-do citizens to dormitory towns in the Gooi and the Kennemerland. The poor and unemployed occupied vacant canal houses, converted them into smaller units and filled them from cellar to loft with their large families. Hygiene left much to be desired, especially because the canals were still used as sewers. Here too the liberals saw the solution in private enterprise, which considering the few powers left to the council under the constitution of 1848, was the only remaining possibility.

The land in the Plantage was released for building on by rich citizens. In 1838 the Natura Artis Magistra society had already built a zoo there. When in 1848 the city ramparts were demolished and a little later the city excises and tolls were abolished, expansion outside the ramparts became possible. The first expansion included the areas on and along the city ramparts on which villas and other buildings were built. By setting up several businesses and by building the Paleis voor Volksvlijt on the Frederiksplein, Dr. Sarphati hoped to reduce unemployment, improve the city and raise the morale of its people. He was the first to propose a building plan for the working class as well as for the wealthy. In the area around the Frederiksplein only the buildings on the Westeinde, the Oosteinde and along the Hemonylaan, together with the majestic Amstel Hotel and the Sarphatistraat which leads over the Hogesluis bridge, are left to remind us of his design.

The demand for houses increased in the rapidly industrializing town and many entrepreneurs followed Sarphati's example. Building activity began around the exit roads but quickly spread throughout the area up to the city boundaries. The city council realized that action was badly needed in order to preserve same vestige of cohesion. In 1866 the city architect Van Niftrik proposed an expansion plan, which, however, met with much criticism because the necessary, compulsory purchase of property did not conform to the liberal ideas of the city council. The plan consisted of a linked succession of working-class areas, villa parks and promenade parks. Many people see the influence of Haussman's plans for Paris in the geometrical street pattern.

In the final plan of 1876 by the director of Public Works Kalff and Van Niftrik, only the Westerpark, the Sarphatipark and the Oosterpark are left to remind us of Van Niftrik's plan. The first two were carried out according to his designs. Apart from the Vondelpark (which was laid out privately), these parks were the only green spaces between the built-up areas. Kalffs plan took property boundaries into account and followed, as in the Jordaan, the alignment of pastures and drainage ditches. The city council assisted with the completion of the street network. This raised street rates and lowered building casts. Because Amsterdam, like so many European cities, made credit available, a real building revolution took place from 1874 till 1900, during which as many houses as possible were built on as little land as possible. The development consisted of closed housing blocks around

Development Plan Amsterdam, 1876, J. Kalff

courtyards in which only the architectural treatment showed the difference in social status between the different houses. Supervision of the building regulations was insufficient, so that many a newly-built block of houses collapsed.

The council accepted responsibility for the infrastructure, but at the end of the 1870's had the builders themselves pay for the roads. Little consideration was paid to the way in which main roads linked up with the old city as the junction of the Overtoom with the Leidseplein shows. The irregular route of the Ceintuurbaan linked the main roads to each other and shows a lay-out that was not very well planned. At the same time the arrival of office blocks and department stores in the city centre made it necessary to fill in many old canals such as the Spui, the Nieuwezijds Voorburgwal and the Nieuwezijds Achterburgwal (now the Spuistraat) in order to create good connections to the Central Station. The houses behind the Palace on the Dam had to be sacrificed for the construction of the Raadhuisstraat. Traffic began to take its toll.

Workers who could afford a new home settled predominantly in the eastern and western parts of the nineteenth century belt, while the better-off moved into houses along the Weteringschans, the Plantage, the Sarphatistraat and, around 1900, the neighbourhood of the Museumplein. Near the Kinkerstraat canals were dug partly to imitate the character of the seventeenth century concentric canals, yet mainly for reasons of hygiene. In addition to the improvement of education and hygiene the housing of unskilled labourers became part of the social question which after 1850 began to play an important role in politics. However, the members of the philanthropically building associations were able to accomplish very little, because they were unwilling to compromise the interests of firms in which they themselves were the major shareholders. Their ideas were to form the basis of the criticism of the Radical Liberals who together with the Confessionals tried to defeat the Liberals. From 1890 onwards their influence was decisive. When in 1896 parts of adjacent municipalities such as Nieuwer Amstel were annexed, the land was leased out and observance of the building regulations was more tightly controlled. Public transport as well as the electricity and gas companies was taken over by the city council. In addition to legislation to improve working conditions the Housing Act was passed in 1901.

The council intervenes

Apart from a slight recession in 1923 the growth of the economy and the increase in population continued until 1929. The Housing Act of 1901 enabled the city authorities to draw up compulsory building regulations and to grant subsidies to house builders, giving preference to housing corporations. Moreover, building materials had become expensive for private individuals. Due to the increasing influence of the local authority in public housing, the Housing Department and Public Works became important institutions and became involved in the debate about town planning theory. The districts around the Lairessestraat and the Willemsparkweg were built on land acquired by annexation. Work was started in the Indische Buurt, the Oosterpark area was completed and the Transvaal

AMSTERDAM

SCHAAL 1:10000

Development Plan
Amsterdam, 1922,
H.P. Berlage

area, in which important architects such as Berlage were involved, was realized. The Transvaalbuurt amounted to a demonstration of the use of town squares. It is possible that same of Berlage's designs were prelim-inary exercises for one of the climaxes of pre-war town planning: the 1917 development plan for Zuid (Amsterdam South).

This Plan Zuid was commissioned by the council to cover a section to the south of the Ceintuurbaan and was carried out in a somewhat revised form. It was the first time that aesthetic considerations had played an important role in planning. By combining wide avenues and winding side-streets, Berlage hoped to achieve the same mixture of the monumental and the picturesque which had character-ized the seventeenth century concentric canals. The avenues lead into squares in which monumental buildings were to have closed the perspective. Instead of artists' residences and an art academy, however, the buildings that were actu-ally built were more mundane. A 'skyscraper' was built in the eastern part at the intersection of the Rooseveltlaan, the Vrijheidslaan and the Churchilllaan.

In the western part, dominated by a trident configuration of streets, a hotel was to appear at the end of the central axis. Owing to the increased traffic,

13

the squares have become busy traffic intersections. Seventy-five percent of all the buildings were intended to be working-class housing, making the plan an expression of the ideas, which were fundamental to the Housing Act. In Berlage's social vision all people were equal and, although the brief demanded a division into classes (the well-to-do came to live in the western part), Berlage was able to bring together the different classes by offering everybody the same environment. The garden city concept, originating in England, was introduced to Amsterdam by socialist councillors such as Wibaut and De Miranda. These ideas were given shape in Tuindorp-Oostzaan, Volenwijk and with the incorporation into Amsterdam of the Watergraafsmeer in Betondorp. The notion of garden suburbs was suggested by fears of megalopolis. In the opinion of architect Van Eesteren and town planner Van Lohuizen of the Town Planning Department, these fears were unfounded. In 1935 they produced the General Development Plan (Algemeen Uitbreidingsplan, AUP). This plan was unique in that it was based on a combination of requirements, resulting from statistical and demographic surveys. Housing, employment, transport and recreation were functions of a town, which deserved equal attention. The designers stated in the AUP of 1935, that Amsterdam would be complete in the year 2000 and would have around 900.000 inhabitants. Before the war, in 1934, a competition for cheap working-class houses was held as part of the AUP. It was won by representatives of the Nieuwe Bouwen (Functionalism). On the basis of their design, housing was built in Bos en Lommer, an area in the western part of the city. The closed block was abandoned in order to admit more sun and air and green areas became more important. The designers were not satisfied with the finished product, however, as the high price of land had compelled the builders to place the façades to a closely together.

Slum-clearance in the Jordaan and the Oostelijke Eilanden, which had been started in the 1920's came to a standstill because of the Depression of 1929. Yet, in the thirties several railways were elevated and in 1939 the Weesperpoortstation was replaced by the more southerly Amstelstation. These actions were intended as part of a scheme for an orbital railway-line around the city. Together with the landscaping of the Amsterdamse Bos (Landscape Park) it was part of a job creation scheme.

After the Second World War: expansion and renewal

When the war was over, the city recovered surprisingly fast. After an initial increase the population now fluctuates around 750.000 but the AUP had not provided for the increase in car ownership and the demand for more living space per inhabitant. The Department of Housing and the Town Planning Department, responsible for most of the new developments, realized that the western suburbs of Geuzenveld, Slotervaart, Slotermeer, Osdorp, Westlandgracht and Buitenveldert in the south were inadequate. Building was also necessary in Amsterdam Noord and Amsterdam Zuid-Oost in the sixties. Flats of more than five storeys appeared for the first time in the north of the city, which in 1968 was connected to the centre by the IJ-tunnel. The Coentunnel and the Schelling-wouderbrug made completion of the ring-road round the city possible and protected Waterland, the polders north of the city, from further expansions. In the AUP the provision of landscaping received as much attention as housing, employment and transport. The layout of the Amsterdamse Bos started before the war and in the fifties suburbs in Amsterdam West were situated around the large Sloterplas (lake).

In the Bijlmermeer in Amsterdam Zuidoost the separation of different types of traffic according to function on different levels formed the structural theme. The area was connected to the centre by the metro. The Bijlmermeer, with its abundant greenery, separate traffic zones, large car parks and centrally situated shops, could have become the triumph of the ideas embodied in the AUP. Reference was also made to the ideas of CIAM. However, the large scale on which the Bijlmermeer was built, incurred much criticism and the district of Gaasperdam was laid out on a smaller scale with low-rise building. The proximity of motorways and railway has made Zuidoost very attractive for the establishment of businesses. It is currently a large office building site. Apart from Schiphol airport and the Zuidas these businesses provide most of the job opportunities.

This development is the opposite of what was happening in the sixties. Then many businesses settled in the city centre and large roads threatened to devastate characteristic parts of the town. Of those large roads only the Wibautstraat was actually built. The construction of the metro, for which many houses were demolished in the Nieuwmarktbuurt (the former Lastage) met with much resistance from the local population. Their opposition led to a turning point in council policy with regard to urban renewal. On which the population now has more influence. The Pentagon in Jodenbreestraat and housing around Nieuwmarkt are successful examples of this development.

Housing and employment in the city centre now receive equal attention, often owing to the neighbourhood action groups. Neighbourhoods eligible for urban renewal are renovated in phases, adhering to the nineteenth century infrastructure. The council now has the difficult task of keeping motor traffic out of the city centre without causing firms to think twice about establishing themselves there. Therefore, public transport is being improved and the use of bicycles stimulated. In 1978 the railway line to Schiphol from Amsterdam Rai Station was opened and in 1986 the second Schiphol railway line, through the western part of the city, was brought into service. After fifty years, the orbital railway line was realised with Amsterdam-Rai station being connected to Duivendrecht station.

In 1985 two unusual plans were completed. For the IJ-plein Rem Koolhaas designed a plan in which urban villas and rows of low-rise buildings are placed in such a way that as many residents as possible have a view of the river IJ. Carel Weeber was responsible for the Venserpolder development, where, with reference to Berlage's Plan Zuid, he built closed housing blocks with large courtyards along wide streets.

Koolhaas' plan generally meets with approval, whereas the plan by Weeber arouses controversy. Both demonstrate that there is still a lively debate about town planning in Amsterdam. The council has plans to build offices, hotels, museums and houses along the river IJ and in the eastern docklands in order to stop the migration from the city centre. This has become a new proving-ground for town-planning ideas.

The compact city

During the 1970s the continued emphasis on urban renewal and social housing led to a large-scale exodus of the better off from Amsterdam. Because there was little opportunity for them to move up the housing ladder, they moved to rapidly growing neighbouring municipalities – initially with the encouragement of Amsterdam itself. Affordable single-family dwellings with gardens were available in these 'overflow municipalities', such as Almere and Purmerend. But the need for people to commute between these growth centres and Amsterdam each day caused enormous traffic problems. Furthermore, this exodus distorted Amsterdam's population structure. Amsterdam was compelled to respond, and policy shifted towards promoting the concept of a 'compact city'. Although with the construction of the Bijlmermeer the municipality considered Amsterdam full, it went looking for new housing locations within the city's boundaries, preferring those that could also offer employment opportunities. By taking over sites abandoned by industry, urban enclaves have been created over the past few years which have their own unique atmosphere and style of architecture. The Oostelijk Havengebied (Eastern Harbour District), which is centrally situated in relation to the city centre, was rediscovered for example. And several hitherto undeveloped areas between the city's western suburbs were earmarked for housing. One example is the market-gardening district of Nieuw-Sloten. Under the terms of a 1988 covenant agreed with the state, a start had to be made on constructing 5767 dwellings in the Oostelijk Havengebied before 1996. The final target envisages the construction of 8500 dwellings housing around 17,000 inhabitants. A total of 33,000 dwellings will have to be built in Amsterdam over the next decade. The development of the Oostelijk Havengebied since the end of the 1980s demonstrates well how the emphasis of municipal policy and town-planning ideas has shifted. Though the earliest projects (along the Cruquiusweg) proposed constructing only social housing, on Java-eiland and Borneo-Sporenburg seventy per cent of all new housing is free-market sector. Of particular interest though are the different architectural approaches taken by the projects, such as The KNSM-eiland, with the much discussed sculptural, brick housing block by the German architect Hans Kollhoff. For the island's remarkable location, in the middle of the IJ, the municipality opted largely for closed blocks in order to create a clear distinction between public and private. This reveals a completely different view from that taken a number of years previously in IJ plein. The architect Jo Coenen was responsible for the detailed urban masterplan for KNSM-eiland. In contrast, Sjoerd Soeters, who drew up the urban design plan for Java-eiland, rejected large freestanding blocks. He wanted the façades to be designed by different architects. In his plan four artificial canals transverse the long narrow island. What Soeters is particularly seeking here is the alternation of sight lines which results as one crosses a steep bridge. Furthermore, the combination of small canal houses and large apartment buildings creates differences of scale and atmosphere.

On Borneo-Sporenburg most houses are single-family dwellings, with a density of around 100 dwellings per hectare. The firm of West 8 drew up the plan and developed a completely new type of dwelling, arranged around a patio, garden or roof terrace. The dwellings are designed by various architects. Large apartment buildings 'rise up' between the streets of terraced houses. These serve to increase the dwelling density, but they also function as 'modern church towers', landmarks amid the low-rise.

Just as with Borneo-Sporenburg, the starting point in the district of Nieuw-Sloten was very high density low-rise. By stacking dwellings in the centre of the area, it was possible for most to be single-family dwellings. Here too, the high-rise served to provide a point of reference for the entire area. A clear structure and a carefully considered design of the public space have encouraged a further improvement in the quality of life in this densely populated area.

Following the Bijlmermeer fiasco, it was clear that good links and services are essential for the success of a new residential location. In this respect Nieuw-Sloten and De Aker are very favourably situated - close to the ring road and Schiphol, but also close to existing services in surrounding areas. A high-speed tram link will connect the city centre (Central Station) with the Oostelijk Havengebied, the ring road and the large, new construction area of IJburg via the Piet Heintunnel. Over the past few years it has been around the World Trade Centre (WTC) and in Amsterdam-Zuidoost that significant concentrations of office space have appeared. Both the prestige offices around the WTC and the ABN AMRO Bank headquarters in the Zuidas are well situated as a result of their proximity to a railway and metro station. Furthermore, a north-south metro line is being build to link the city to Amsterdam-Noord. A large office park has also been established close to Bijlmer Station in the past few years, in combination with the modernisation of the shopping centre 'Amsterdamse Poort'. The construction of the Arena-stadium was a major stimulus to the further development of the area.

New plans for a wide IJ-boulevard along Amsterdam's waterfront, providing space for offices, dwellings and cultural organizations are in development. Amsterdam will continue to expand by building housing on new artificial islands in the IJmeer, outside the ring road, in Amsterdam North and the 'Zuidas', which shows that, fuelled by new ideas, the intense debate on town planning is continuing to rage in Amsterdam.

Parks in Amsterdam

On a recent street map of Amsterdam one is immediately struck by two colours, green and blue. Blue represents the history of Amsterdam from when the city was founded on the spot where the rivers Amstel and IJ converge. The canals, waterways and lakes all have a history of their own. They are all from a later date, as are the cemeteries, public parks and gardens. Indeed, public parks and gardens became common only during the course of the nineteenth century. Together with the roads, squares, façades and water, public green space has become the determining factor in the quality of public space in the city. Amsterdam's landscape depicts a special situation.

Within the ring of canals

The planting illustrated on the well-known map by Cornelis Anthonisz. from 1544 is confined to a few vegetable gardens and orchards belonging to monasteries. Vegetables, fruits and herbs were grown there. The Begijnhof between Kalverstraat and Spui dates from 1346 but was later extended. Most of Amsterdam's hofjes were founded during the seventeenth and eighteenth centuries as almshouses. In 1610 plans were made to construct the famous ring of concentric canals, and the scheme was further elaborated in Daniël Stalpaert's map of 1665. A striking feature of this scheme was the canals lined with trees on both sides. As is evident from poems, travel stories, paintings and charters, great importance was attached to green space in the city's expansion. A stadsgaardenier (city gardener) was responsible for the trees in the city and for any new planting.

At that time, the authorities also regulated private gardens along the canals. On 19 November 1615 an ordinance was enacted which laid down conditions under which land was granted along parts of Herengracht and Keizersgracht. Local regulations permitted the owner of a plot to build on an area up to 100 Amsterdamsche voeten (1 voet is 28 cm) from the street. In addition, a summerhouse was permitted at the end of the property as long as it was no more than 15 voeten deep. The space in between was left unbuilt and intended for a garden. The seventeenth-century architect Philips Vingboons designed a number of canal houses with adjoining geometrical gardens in which the same elements are present namely vegetable gardens, parterres de broderie (embroidered parterres), bleaching grounds, summerhouses and aviaries. Even now, a number of luxuriant examples of this wealth of planting and of the sculptures and summerhouses exist. From 1880 onwards the landscape architect L.A. Springer remodelled a number of canal gardens into country-house gardens according to the fashion of the time. From 1920 onwards J.R. Koning restored a number of properties (keurblokken) along the lines of seventeenth-century geometrical designs. The reconstructed private gardens of the Museum Willet-Holthuysen and Museum van Loon, with its beautiful summerhouse, also have a markedly architectural structure.

Apart from having a canal house, wealthy owners often had an estate in the country or along the rivers Amstel or Vecht. By about 1700 there were about 400 such estates around Amsterdam, along the Amstel, the Haarlemmerweg, in Watergraafsmeer, in Kennemerland and in the Vecht region.

With the exception of Herengracht and Nieuwe Herengracht the concentric ring of canals terminates at the Plantage in the east of the city. In 1682 the authorities decided to situate a pleasure garden between Nieuwe Herengracht, Plantage Muidergracht and Plantage Doklaan. This was the first sizeable green open space in Amsterdam. The architect J. Bosch divided the rectangular site into straight lanes along which privately owned gardens and places to relax were situated. The area became an important attraction and was, until 1940, a thriving entertainment centre. Even though part of the Plantage was built on in the nineteenth century, Artis (the zoo), founded in 1839 on the initiative of three individuals, continued to occupy most of the area.

Walking to the Plantage from the city via Plantage Middenlaan, one sees on the right the aid Hortus Botanicus (the botanical gardens), established here in 1682, and, on the left, Wertheimpark, named in 1898 after the banker A.C. Wertheim. The park along Nieuwe Herengracht was laid out in 1812 by the civic architect A. van der Hart and was originally part of a larger site which included what is now a sports field behind the park.

Parks outside the ramparts

The gardens laid out on both sides of the Willemspoort in 1843 were enlarged two years later with a park on 't Blauwhoofd, a city fortification. This created a popular promenade to the river IJ and offered the city's inhabitants a magnificent view towards the river Zaan and the Zuiderzee from near the present Houtmankade. Despite being extended in the direction of the Bogt (another fortification) in 1857, Park Blauwhoofd's existence was short-lived. The park disappeared in 1869 when a connecting canal was dug. These developments meant the city's outer limits had been breached however.

Park Blauwhoofd still featured in J.G. van Niftrik's famous 1866 expansion plan for Amsterdam. He planned a number of working-class neighbourhoods, urban-villa neighbourhoods and city parks in a new strip along Singelgracht. By 1855 responsibility for planting trees in the city was vested in the newly established Dienst van Publieke Werken (Public Works Department). Thus Van Niftrik, as civic engineer, had considerable influence on both urban development as well as the layout of green open space.

Amsterdam's most famous park, Vondelpark, was a private initiative however. In its current state, little now remains of another private initiative, that by Samuel Sarphati, a doctor, who designed a luxurious, green residential district in Amsterdam's Oud-Zuid. The Sarphatipark (1885) is a vague memorial to Sarphati's intentions. Westerpark was probably designed by Van Niftrik and laid out in 1891 on the site where, fifty years before, the first steam train left for Haarlem. This park and Oosterpark, which was completed in 1894 by the landscape architect L.A. Springer, were included in the urban-expansion plan drawn up in 1876 by the new director of the Public Works Department, J. Kalff. The smaller public gardens like Frederiksplein (1870) and Frederik Hendrikplantsoen (1883) outside the Singelgracht often included references to the planting at the former gates to the city. Some of the trees in the Leidsche Bosjes date from before the Leidsepoort demolished in 1862.

Green space in large-scale urban development

At the beginning of the twentieth century Amsterdam had relatively little public green space in comparison with foreign cities. The tact was noted by a committee from the Amsterdamse Woningraad (Amsterdam Housing Board) and included in the Rapport over de Amsterdamse Parken en Plantsoenen (Report on the Parks and Public Gardens of Amsterdam). To improve the situation proposals were put forward by, among others, the architect H.P. Berlage and the conservationist Jac.P. Thijsse. Thijsse wanted to link the centre of Amsterdam with the pol-ders outside the city by means of four green axes. Thijsse played a prominent role in setting up the Vereniging tot Behoud van Natuurmonumenten (Association for the Preservation of Nature Reserves). With the purchase in 1906 of Naardermeer near Amsterdam, the first nature reserve was established. The need for green open space led local SDAP (Social Democratic Labour Party) councillors to provide the city's first playgrounds and allotments. In about 1915 the IJbos (later renamed after the socialist councillor W.H. Vliegen: Vliegenbos) and Volewijkspark were laid out in Amsterdam-Noord. The important routes in Berlage's Plan Zuid such as Apollolaan also show how, from the 1920s, the municipal authorities took seriously their responsibility for providing public space. In 1926 a start was made on laying out the Zuiderzeepark (Flevopark) along the Nieuwe Diep, followed by the Beatrixpark in 1938.

The green connecting links propagated by Thijsse can be recognized in the Algemeen Uitbreidingsplan (1934), which included the 900-ha Amsterdamse Bos, and in the later struggle to preserve the green banks of the Amstel. In the case of major housing projects in and around Amsterdam, the Vaste Commissie voor Uitbreidingsplannen (Standing Committee on Extension Plans) gave detailed advice and paid considerable attention to the relationship between city and nature.

These new ideals also resulted in the provision of communal green spaces between blocks of houses. A good example of this is the communal garden designed by the landscape architect Mien Ruys at Geuzenhof, a 1930s public-housing project on Willem de Zwijgerlaan. The garden, which opened out onto the lower gallery of the block, included a stage for performing music and plays, an ornamental pool, an aviary and sandboxes. The garden was planted with simple indigenous plants. Ruys has designed many projects in Amsterdam which are worth a visit. They include communal gardens for housing in Frankendaal (De Sitterstraat, 1949), which has a playground by Aldo van Eyck and the small park at what used to be the offices of the KNSM (KNSM-laan, around 1950) and which she herself has recently adapted as part of the development of the Oostelijk Havengebied.

Most parks suffered considerably during the Second World War and profound renovations were necessary. This provided an opportunity to further elaborate the recreational function given to parks as an integral component in the design process by the Algemeen Uitbreidingsplan. The prominence of Sloterplas in the Westelijke Tuinsteden and of Gijsbrecht van Aemstelpark in Buitenveldert is indicative of a more intense interaction. Rembrandtpark (1973), plans for which had been drawn up even before the Second World War, links the older neighbourhood De Baarsjes, which dates from the period of the Amsterdam School, with the flats in the Overtoomse Veld. Existing parks, such as the Westerpark and Noorderpark, were renovated, expanded and modernised, and new parks, such as Diemerpark, were built.

In order to solve the problem of a lack of recreational facilities, in the 1960s the government resolved to lay out 'green stars', and larger areas close to the city were redesigned as places of recreation. It was as a result of this policy that Het Twiske to the north of Amsterdam and Spaarnwoude between Amsterdam, Velsen and Haarlem were developed. The high point of the green-city concept was reached in the 1960s when the Bijlmermeer was built. High-rise flats were built in a wooded landscape divided into so-called woonhoven (residential courts), local parks and large, green open spaces like Gaasperplas. The park at Gaasperplas was the result of the International Horticultural Exhibition, the Floriade, which was held in Amsterdam for the second time in 1982. In 1972 Amstelpark was laid out for the same purpose.

Recent urban-development schemes of Nieuw-Sloten and the Oostelijk Havengebied illustrate a new vision in municipal policy towards green space. The landscape architect Lodewijk Baljon was supervisor for the architecture and public space in Nieuw-Sloten, which should be densely built but also retain an open character. Those who conceived the layout of the Oostelijk Havengebied (West 8 landscape architects) and the IJ lake started from the proposition that 'blue is green'.

Since the end of the 1990s a wave of innovation has given public space in the heart of Amsterdam and the islands a whole different appearance. Historically important squares have received new pavement, lighting and street furniture. The Danish landscape architect Sven-Ingvar Andersson was responsible for the design and execution of the Museumplein.

Frankendael
c. 1660 5.3 ha
Rebuilding 1997-2004

This seventeenth-century farmstead in the impoldered Watergraafsmeer was converted into a country estate during the eighteenth century. In 1835 it became a popular pleasure garden for the people of Amsterdam. Its attractions included a playground, a tearoom and an island with a hermitage set between poplar trees. In 1867 the Koninklijke Nederlandsche Tuinbouw Maatschappij 'Linnaeus' acquired Frankendaal and founded a nursery and a horticultural school. One of its students was the well-known landscape architect Leonard Springer. The municipality of Amsterdam subsequently became the owner and established the city's nurseries here in 1886. H.C. Zwart, head of the city's parks department and later, from 1923, J.R. Koning lived on the estate. In 1925 an open-air theatre was built in the woods behind the house, and two years later the first mass open-air lessons for children began. In the 1930s the school gardens and an allotment complex were added. The botanical garden was laid out by J. Jongsma in 1960. In 1982 this historic country estate became a public park. The Louis-XVI-style entrance gate is embellished at the front with Ionic pilasters, ferns and a medallion with the head of Mercury (Jacob Otten Husly, 1783). There is a fountain in a shell-shaped basin representing the sea-god Poseidon and his wife, the sea nymph Amphritite, a small boy sitting on a dolphin plays the lyre (Van Logteren, 1714). Buro Sant & Co has taken responsibility for the design and realisation (1997-2004) of the renewal of the park. One of the pleasantest additions is the 'Eettuin De Kas' in the middle of the park. The historic garden near the house is a reconstruction by Lucia Albers.

Hortus Botanicus
1682
1.7 ha

After the Plantage had been laid out on the edge of the old city, there was space over for the new Hortus Medicus. The plants and seeds supplied by the Dutch East India Company and the West India Company enabled an extraordinary collection of exotic plants to be built up. The semicircular hedges and the flowerbeds are a reference to the seventeenth century. Later the Hortus was used as a research garden for the University of Amsterdam. The iron palm house on Plantage Kerklaan dates from 1912. A major renovation began in the late 1980s. The tropical hothouse, which consists of three separate glasshouses each with a different climate, was completed in 1993 to a design by Zwarts & Jansma architects and laid out by landscape architect Wybe Kuitert. A fine collection of old trees in Wertheimpark on the other side of Plantage Middenlaan recalls the period when the park was part of the Hortus.

Vondelpark
J.D. Zocher & L.P. Zocher, 1864-1865 8 ha
L.P. Zocher, 1877 40 ha

The park was laid out in the rustic area between Singelgracht and Amstelveenseweg on the initiative of the Amsterdam banker C.P. van Eeghen (1816-1889).
Up to 1953 Vondelpark was in private hands. The park was designed in two
phases. The layout by Jan David Zocher jun. (1791-1870) and his son Louis
Paul (1820-1915), both from a famous family of park designers, consists of
meandering paths, pools and small graves alternating with open fields.
The original plan envisaged exotic plants. During the past century the park has
been repeatedly adapted to reflect the needs of the time. During the summer
the park is crowded with tourists and people from the city. Vondelpark is to be
the first public park in the Netherlands to be listed as a national monument. See
320 for the buildings and sculptures.

Zorgvlied
J.D. Zocher jun. & L.P. Zocher, 1867-1869
L.P. Zocher, 1891-1892
C.P. Broerse, 1967 14 ha

This cemetery is an enclave of the municipality of Amstelveen and lies along the
banks of the river Amstel. The oldest part dates from 1867 and, like the extension
in 1891-1892, is laid out in the landscape style. The most recent extension, by
C.P. Broerse (1902-1995), is laid out in a more rigid 'Roman' style. The monuments are situated amidst poplars, weeping willows and dark coniferous trees,
which provide an appropriate mood. There are fine monuments to be seen, like
the family tomb of Oscar Carré (1891, by J.P.F. van Rossem and W.J. Vuyk, also
the architects of Circustheater Carré, 1887), and the last resting place of many
famous Amsterdam personalities, such as the architect Eduard Cuypers (1927),
sculptor Hildo Krop (1970) and the painter Carel Willink (1983). See also 316.

Sarphatipark
J.G. van Niftrik, 1881-1886 4.5 ha

Little became of plans by Samuel Sarphati (1813-1866) for a salubrious residential district near Ceintuurbaan. In J. Kalff's extension plans for the city, only
4.5 ha (the equivalent of two building blocks in the urban grid) were devoted
to creating a municipal park. The park has a meandering footpath linking the
ponds, as well as typical landscape elements such as idyllic bridges and a small
waterfall. On the other side of the park, which is at polder water level, water
was pumped by what used to be a steam-driven pumping station (opposite the
entrance to the park at the end of Eerste Jan van der Heijdenstraat) and drained
off into the Boerenwetering. The playground was a later addition. During the
restoration of Sarphatipark in 1994 the paths were raised, the southern part was
given a more wooded character and the north was replanted with ornamental
shrubs and perennials. For the Sarphati monument see 336.

Amsterdamse Bos
Jacoba Mulder & Cor van Eesteren, 1931-1937
Layout 1934-1970
900 ha

In 1928 the municipality of Amsterdam decided to lay out a park between the Nieuwe Meer, the ring canal of the Haarlemmermeerpolder and Amstelveenseweg. A Bos commission consisting of a large number of experts on the natural environment urban development, recreation and landscape architecture was asked to investigate how best to develop the park. On their advice, the land along the shores of the older veenplassen of the Poel and the Nieuwe Meer was preserved. Most of the extensive recreational facilities were to be located in the middle of the park. The park was to be planted along geographical lines with trees indigenous to the forests of Western Europe. It was laid out as part of the Algemeen Uitbreidingsplan according to a design by the architects Cor van Eesteren (1897-1988) and Jacoba Mulder (1900-1988). Mulder was responsible for the design and execution of the Bosplan, which provided for equal areas given over to forest, open space and water. A 300-km-long pipe-drainage system formed the basis of the park, which in some places is 5.5 m below sea level. From the artificial hill, the highest point, there are fine sight lines to the mostly landscaped layout with its curved paths, ponds and alternately open fields and thick forests. All types of sport are represented. The separate paths for ramblers, cyclists and horse riders are functional. There is also a hockey stadium, a camping site, and the Bosbaan, a wide canal used for boat races. The farmhouse Meerzicht has been transformed into a restaurant. Between 1937 and 1945 the Amsterdam School architect P.L. Kramer designed about fifty wooden bridges for the park; they vary in shape and detail. About 20.000 unemployed worked on this park since the 1930s as part of a relief-work project.

Jac.P. Thijssepark
Design and layout C.P. Broerse, 1940-1972
5.3 ha

To visit one of Amsterdam's finest parks one has to cross into Amstelveen. This neighbouring municipality is well known for the high quality of its green open space. The former head of the city's parks department C.P. Broerse made an important contribution to this. The Jac.P. Thijssepark, named after the founder of the Vereniging tot Behoud van Natuurmonumenten, is situated between Amsterdamseweg and the Amsterdamse Bos and was inspired by the traditional Dutch peat landscape. The mostly indigenous planting is grouped around smaller enclosed beds in which the traditional lawn is replaced by herbs. Other botanical parks in Amstelveen such as Braak, Landwehrpark and Meander are also worth a visit.

Jac. P. Thijssepark

Gijsbrecht van Aemstelpark
Design and layout W.C.J. Boer, 1959-1962
c. 40 ha

A narrow green strip in Buitenveldert links the Amsterdamse Bos with Amstelpark over a length of two kilometres. Wim Boer was one of the few landscape architects to join the Opbouw architects and the influence of that movement can be seen in his design. By continuing the pattern of the housing blocks in the geometrical design of the park, he produced an impressive integration of urban development and park architecture. The paths link up with the street layout of the area, and much use has been made of asphalt, concrete and stone. Near the shopping centre in the centre of the green strip is an island, intended as a place to meet. This square is enclosed by flower-beds, a pergola and a rectangular pond. A restaurant has been built on a peninsula to the east of the central square. A wide promenade lined with plane-trees runs parallel to Van Nijenrodeweg.

The town garden of Museum Willet-Holthuysen
Design Egbert Mos
Renovation Saskia Albrecht
Opened 1972
770 m²

Following a fire in 1929 Amstelstraat 20 and 22 lay fallow. The site had been obtained by the municipality of Amsterdam partly as the result of a legacy from the Willet-Holthuysen couple. A gift from a bank for the purpose of improving Rembrandtplein was used in part to lay out a garden behind the Museum Willet-Holthuysen. This town garden was to be in the French classical style once popular in eighteenth-century Holland. It was laid out in 1972 by E. Mos, head of the city's parks department. Only a few plant types are used in this symmetrical garden. The central parterres constist of clipped box hedges and red and white gravel. They are bordered by a grass verge. Pear trees have been planted and these are trained against the trellises. As well as having an eighteenth-century sundial, the garden is embellished with a series of sculptures by Ignatius van Logteren dating from 1721 and representing Flora, the goddess of flowers and spring, and Pomona, the goddess of fruit.

Erasmuspark
Egbert Mos 1960-1961
Renovated 2003
11 ha

There were gardens on this site even before the Second World War. Jan van Galenpark was situated here in the period after 1926. The present park to the north of Jan van Galenstraat in the Bos en Lommer district was completed only in the 1960s and reconstructed recently by Urban van Aar. Admiralengracht broadens out along one side of the park and then flows into Erasmusgracht. Erasmuspark is laid out as a polder and has a geometrical structure enclosed by a dike to the north and the east. The water level in the park is the same as the polder water level, a few meters below NAP (the Dutch ordnance datum). The water in the surrounding canals is kept at the maximum level of the boezem, the polder outlets. The bridge across Admiralengracht along Jan van Galenstraat was built in 1933 to a design by Piet Kramer. The series of four sculptures by Hildo Krop (of an Eskimo with seals, an American stockbroker, a Negro with lions and a Chinese) represent the four points of the compass. Next to the steps and the incline leading to the path on the ring-dike around the park are two statues by J. Klaas (Mother and Child) and H. van Lith (Nude Standing).

Museumplein
Design Sven-Ingvar Andersson in cooperation with Stefan Gall
(Atelier Quadrat, 1992-1995)
Completed 2001

Many plans have been drawn up over the past hundred years for this large triangular space behind the Rijksmuseum. In 1884 a garden was laid out around the museum according to a design by P.J.H. Cuypers, the Rijksmuseum's architect. It was designed in an eclectic style and functioned as a sort of outdoor museum, containing, among other things, fragments of old buildings, city gates and gates to country estates which had been removed from their original locations, statues, arbours and pollard trees. Despite the many designs for villas and parks, Museumplein has remained an open space. The idea of having a garden here continued to live on, however, and new plans were recently drawn up for the site. The design by the Danish architect Sven-Ingvar Andersson (pupil of C.Th. Sørensen) preserves the openness of the square, but the 1952 layout by the city's Public Works Department with the 'shortest motorway in the Netherlands', disappeared. Instead, meadows, a pedestrian area, a pond and diagonally arranged rows of trees are created. One of the most attractive features is the sloping expanse of grass near the Stedelijk Museum. During summer evenings Andersson's light design gives the square a most urban character. In 2011 the Stedelijk opens its exeptional extension fronting on the Museumplein, designed by Benthem Crouwel.

Museumplein

Westerpark and Westergasfabriek
Design by Kathryn Gustafson-Neil Porter (USA/UK) 1997-2003,
Extension of 13.5 ha

This project for the rebuilding of the former gasometer terrain into a recreational park was complex. Thirteen buildings including the gasometer were renovated for the park. Since its opening in 2003 there are multiple ponds with planting of various kinds, restaurant and cafe facilities and a children's play pond, among other things. Much attention was given in the design to water features alternating with plazas and a field for events. The attention paid to planting can be seen in the selection of various species of trees and perennials. The starting point for the detailing and the selection of lighting was the large volume of visitors. Quite in the Dutch tradition, along the railway line various levels have been constructed, with embankments reminiscent of dikes. The new design links up with the landscaped section of the Westerpark, laid out in the 19th century.

Noorderpark

Noorderpark
Design by West 8 Urban Design & Landscape Architecture
2011

Noorderpark is a new park facility that was created after the consolidation of Florapark and Volewijkspark, both designed in the English landscape style. In the design the landscape architect Adriaan Geuze put the park's social function first. He made no radical interventions in the contours and organisation of the existing parks; in his own words, the architect wanted only to 'kiss them awake' by connecting the parts of the parks with one another and better utilising the existing elements. The new design particularly emphasises the long sight lines – referring to the vistas of the North Holland landscape.

Before 1700

The first houses of Amsterdam were made of wood and consisted of three aisles. These houses were similar to the timber buildings still existing in Amsterdam Noord. Fairly early a more intensive land-use led to the adoption of a two-aisled type. At the end of the fourteenth and the beginning of the fifteenth century the one-aisled house that is so typical of the architecture of Amsterdam came into existence. Thus, the finished product was determined by local circumstances: narrow, deep and increasingly tall houses with steep roofs. The houses built with timber frames and thatched roofs, had timber gables with each floor jutting out in order to throw rainwater clear of the façade. In the fifteenth century bricks increasingly took over the place of timber. Owing to the risk of fire, a demand for safety measures arose. At first the timber side walls were replaced by brick ones, leaving the rest in timber. At the beginning of the sixteenth century the thatched roofs, which at first were coated with clay, were replaced by tiles. This was regulated by means of statutes (building regulations laid down by the city council). The timber gables too were gradually replaced by brick ones. In 1544 half of all the buildings still had timber gables. Two have survived up to now. The timber lower fronts were retained longest. In the middle of the seventeenth century Philips Vingboons was still designing buildings with lower fronts in timber. The earliest type of brick house was the house with a spout-gable, a literal translation of the timber house into the brick one, with projecting copings to throw water clear of the façade. An alternative to this was the simple step-gable.

Renaissance

The point of departure in the Renaissance is the building as an aesthetic unit derived from human proportions. Each part with its own dimensions and proportions forms a harmonious unity with the building, and so a consistent system of proportions forms the basis of a renaissance building. To achieve this thorough knowledge of the classical world of design was essential. In the second half of the sixteenth century pattern books by Serlio (1475-1545) for example, which were translated into Dutch, were relied upon in the Netherlands. In addition, pattern books by Dutchmen, such as Hans Vredeman de Vries (1527-1606) which had much influence in the Netherlands, were published shortly afterwards. His typical decoration was the strap and scroll ornament, derived from framing resembling incised and curled leather.

The typical step-gable, determined by the steep roof was a non-classical element that had to be absorbed into the ornamentation of the renaissance façade. The solution was an architecture with much emphasis on functional and constructively protective parts: in the relieving arches above wall openings, niche fillings, stringcourses in the brickwork and the gable endings with strap and scroll work, volutes, vases, escutcheons and masks. The space between the windows denoted pilasters, the space under the windows, whether or not in combination with stringcourses determined the entablature. The culminating point of the Renaissance coincides with the period of architect Hendrick de Keyser (1565-1621) and his apparently decorative and playful façade architecture. The combination of the soft, red brick and yellow Bentheimer sandstone embellishment produces a clear and multicoloured imagery of construction and decoration: decoration constructively essential to protect the soft brickwork against the influence of rain. The renaissance step-gable architecture continues until the end of the seventeenth century.

Classicism

In the meantime a stricter conception of the use of classical elements was perceptible. Classicism began around 1625. Classical elements such as pilasters, entablatures and pediments were applied in such a manner that the façade was constructed in an apparently well-ordered manner. Again, Italian books of the orders, especially those by Scamozzi (1615), were used for this purpose. Pediments also made their appearance in architecture. The original function of the classical pediment is after all a covering and enclosing protection against rain and was, therefore, accepted as the means of capping gable ends and protecting windows. In the meantime the soft, red brick was replaced by a harder, brown brick. Through the use of pilasters, entablatures and pediments together with the introduction of a central emphasis by means of a central salient or pavilion, the step-gable changed, through the raised neck-gable (with rudimentary steps) into a neck-gable. At the same time a new decorative element appeared in the façade: the scroll. Where the raised neck-gable still had many fruit and flower ornaments, the neck-gable had many human and animal figures in the scrolls.

The larger and broader houses and the double houses began to resemble temple fronts: one or more tiers of pilasters with entablatures capped by a pediment and of ten decorated with garlands and festoons under the windows.

The most important architect of the first period was Jacob van Campen (1595-1657), who built the Town Hall on the Dam. Later Philips Vingboons (1607-1678) and his brother Justus (1620-1698) appeared.

After 1665 austerity made its appearance: base, pilasters and festoons disappeared. Instead, balconies and attics, sometimes sculptured, appeared. Emphasis was now on the harmony of parts and refinement of execution. The great architect of restrained Dutch Classicism was Adriaan Dortsman (1625-1682).

Church-building

In the building of churches other influences played a role. For years Catholic churches had been built in the Gothic style with the altar as the dominant element. Even before the middle of the sixteenth century we see renaissance motifs and ornaments appear in the Gothic world of design. In the third quarter of the sixteenth century the breakthrough of the renaissance took place, as can be seen in the stained-glass windows and the purely classical architecture in the tower and the chapter house of the Oude Kerk. After the iconoclasm of 1566 the Alteratie took place in 1578, prohibiting the Catholic Church which took recourse in the building of schuilkerken (secret churches) in private houses. The Lutherans and religious groups other than the ruling Dutch reformed were allowed to build churches, but without towers. The choir and the altar ceased to have a function in public worship and the pulpit became dominant. The renaissance ideal of centralized building could now be put into practice. The Zuiderkerk was the first church in Amsterdam to be built for the Dutch Reformed community; a renaissance church, which follows the structural system of the Oude Kerk with timber trusses. As a result of the expansion of the city, the Westerkerk was built for the wealthy bourgeoisie who lived along the canals; on plan similar to the Zuiderkerk, but with a new structural concept. At the same time the Noorderkerk was built as a chapel for the poor who lived in the Jordaan. This truly centralised building was geared to a service in which the pulpit was dominant, whereas the structure is, again, traditional with timber trusses. Classicism continued with centralized buildings as can be seen in the Oosterkerk and the Ronde Lutherse Kerk.

Oudekerksplein 23
1300 onwards Oude Kerk

The oldest part of this church, dedicated to St. Nicholas, is the tower which dates from 1300. In about 1505 several additions in the renaissance style were made by Joost Jansz. Bilhamer. From being a single-aisled church it developed, firstly, to a hall-church and, secondly, to a basilica. It has a rich interior with stained-glass windows of 1555 in the Mariakapel (Lady Chapel) by Dirk Crabeth and Lambert van Noort.

101 centre ☐

Nieuwezijds Voorburgwal 143/Dam
From the end of the
14th century – Nieuwe Kerk

The result of a development beginning at the end of the 14th century, resulting in a late Gothic transept-basilica with ambulatory and radiating chapels. The church has timber and stone vaulting and an unfinished tower by Jacob van Campen. Inside can be seen the tomb of Michiel de Ruyter by Rombout Verhulst (1681), the copper choir screen rail by Lutma (1650) and the pulpit by Vinckenbrinck (1647).

102 centre ☐

Begijnhof 34
1460

Although the whole of the Begijnhof dates from roughly the same period, number 34 is the only one to retain its original timber gable. The timber structure of the house is also present in the other houses. They, however, have been provided with brick gables. The first floor was used for living and was reached by means of an external stair.

103 centre ☐

Prins Hendrikkade 94-95
1480 Schreierstoren

One of the defensive towers of the first city walls. The windows, doors and plaques are later additions. Characteristic is the round-arched frieze on which the battlements were formerly placed.

104 centre ☐

Nieuwmarkt 4
1488 St. Antoniespoort

The main building is flanked by heavy round towers. The city side has octagonal staircase towers. In 1545 it was altered by Alexander Pasqualini and Willem Dirksz. In 1617 it was converted to the Waag (Public Weigh house). In 1691 it was used to house the dissecting room of the Guild of Surgeons. Note the brick bonding in the Bricklayers' Guild room.

105 centre ☐

Zeedijk 1
c. 1550

This timber house has brick sidewalls and a brick rear elevation, providing stability for the timber structure. The front façade has lost its original appearance (the lower front was replaced in the nineteenth century). However, it still gives a good impression of a medieval house. It is now part of a hotel complex.

106 centre ■

Oudezijds Voorburgwal 300
1550 Pakhuis Oudezijds Huiszittenmeesters

Two early examples of spout-gables. The original function of these warehouses was the storage of goods. In 1616 Hendrick de Keyser converted them into the pawnbroker's, which it still is. In 1669 it was extended with an austere, and for its time, modern building. The entrance gate with the city's coat of arms is somewhat in the style of Hendrick de Keyser.

107 centre ■

St. Annenstraat 12
1565 Gulden Trip

This is the only small house surviving from the middle of the 16th century. The top is decorated with strap work and c-shaped volutes in the style of Hans Vredeman de Vries. The window frames are flush with the brickwork, which, unusually for Amsterdam, is executed in Flemish bond.

108 centre ■

Kalverstraat 92
Pieter de Keyser, Jacob van Campen and others
1570 Burgerweeshuis

Orphanage with an entrance gate of 1581 by Joost Jansz. Bilhamer. The boy's courtyard dates from 1632. It has a loggia with 14 Doric columns, bearing shallow spring stones and triglyph consoles. The girls' courtyard of 1634 was executed in giant Ionic. Currently houses the Amsterdam Historical Museum (B. van Kasteel, 1975)

109 centre ☐

Singel 140-142
Hendrick de Keyser
1600 Vergulde Dolphijn

Lively façade owing to the mixture of stringcourses, spring stones, key stones, masks, volutes and obelisks all in white sandstone and the hard, red brickwork. The façade of this building, in which Frans Banningh Cocq, commander of Rembrandt's Nightwatch lived, is capped by two linked double step-gables.

110 centre ■

Zandstraat 17
Hendrick de Keyser
1603 Zuiderkerk

A pseudo-basilica six bays long, with Tuscan columns, timber barrel vaults and dormers. It has a richly, detailed tower, which can be seen clearly from the Groenburgwal: a square stone substructure, on which an octagonal sandstone section stands with free-standing columns on the corners. On the top of this is a wooden, lead-dressed spire. Now an information centre for urban renewal.

111 centre ☐

Oudezijds Voorburgwal 14
1605 Burcht van Leiden

The upper storeys of this broad stepped gable with its simple stone decorations overhang the lower storey. The frieze above the wooden lower front of the building has the lion's masks, to which the building owes its other name of Leeuwenburg, and a stone tablet with the coat of arms of the city of Riga, the client's original home.

112 centre ■

Nieuwmarkt 20-22
1605

The stone details all project from the brickwork, causing a play of shadows over the façade of this double step gabled house. The fine 17th century looking lower fronts of the building are not original; they had cross-windows, similar to the first floor, with the entrance in the middle.

113 centre ■

Oude Hoogstraat 24
Hendrick de Keyser (attrib.)
1605 Oostindisch Huis

The richly detailed entrance is constructed form cushion blocks and has a round window over a door surrounded by volutes. It is flanked by cross windows, above which the tympani have volutes and masks. The crown is a rarity: an ensemble of volutes, scrolls, stone-dressed window openings and a balustrade. The building was built as the head-quarters and administrative offices for the Amsterdam Chamber of the Dutch United East India Company (VOC).

114 centre □

Singel 423
Hendrick de Keyser
1606 Bus- of Tuighuis

Richly decorated trapezium-shaped
gable with volutes, triglyph pilasters,
lion's masks, scrolls and a straight
cornice with orbs. A modern façade
for its time owing to the lack of
stringcourses. It was used as a store
for gunpowder and arms. Nowadays
part of the University of Amsterdam
Library.

115 centre ☐

Oude Waal/Oude Schans 2
Hendrick de Keyser
1606 Montelbaanstoren

The lowest part dates from 1512 and
was part of the defences along the
Oude Schans. On this Hendrick de
Keyser built an octagonal section
and a lead-dressed open-work timber
steeple (also called Mallejan), which
much resembles the tower of the
Oude Kerk.

116 centre ■

Oudezijds Voorburgwal 22
Hendrick de Keyser (attrib.)
Early 17th century
Int Slodt Egmondt

In this façade, cartouches link twin pilasters on which are set stone accolade arches and masks. On the finely carved beam over the timber lower front rests a frieze with two lion's masks and a stone tablet depicting Egmond Castle. The top section of the façade is of a later date.

117 centre ■

Oudezijds Voorburgwal 249/
Grimburgwal/
Oudezijds Achterburgwal
Claes Adriaensz.
1610 Huis op de drie Grachten

The front façade has a strong horizontal articulation caused by the sandstone strips. The cross-windows are placed in semicircular niches. All three façades are closed by a simple stepped gable. In the restoration of 1910 elements which have been lost in previous alterations were restored.

118 centre □

Waterlooplein 211
Willem de Keyser
1654 Huiszittenaalmoeseniershuis

This simple façade has a central pavilion with cornice (brickwork frieze) and pediment. The governors' room with fireplace and decoration scheme are still present. Currently houses the Academie van Bouwkunst (Architectural Academy). In the front two spout-gables and a trapezium-shaped gable with balustrade. Horizontal emphasis given by stone stringcourses, vertical emphasis by means of the openings. Between 2004 and 2006 the interior was radically rebuilt by Claus and Kaan Architects.

119 centre ☐

Koestraat 20
Hendrick Gerritsz.
1611 Vergulde Leeuwshooft

The oldest known neck-gables, in which the stone scrolls, call to mind the scroll-like infill of stepped gables. In 1633 it served as the wine-merchants' guild house. A statue of their patron saint, St. Urbanus, stands in the broken pediment of the entrance gate, designed by Pieter de Keyser.

120 centre ■

Kattegat 4/6
1614 Gouden en Zilveren
Spiegel

Two simple stepped gables with
pilasters at the summit. The cross-
windows are placed flush with the
façade and have arches with spring
stones and keystones which are
made from the same yellow bricks
as make up the horizontal bands
in the façade, rather than from the
usual sandstone.

121 centre ☐

Herengracht 120
1615 Coningh van Denemarken

This façade is almost in its original
state, with a central entrance which
was decorated at a later date.
Functional stringcourses take
advantage of the shape of the
stepped gable with its volute scrolls.
The balustrade on the second float
suggests a greater façade width.

122 centre ■

Haarlemmerstraat 75
1615 Kleine Vleeshal/
Westindisch Huis

Only the elevations of the courtyard
retain their 17th century appearance.
In 1623 the building was rented
to the West Indische Compagnie,
to which it owes its present name.
In 1647 the Nieuwezijds Heren-
logement was established here.
It was rebuilt to house the Lutheran
Orphanage in 1826. It has recently
been restored and is now used for
weddings.

123 centre ☐

Oudezijds Voorburgwal 57
Hendrick de Keyser
1615 Gecroonde Raep

Stepped gable divided horizontally
by cornices, which serve as stringcourses. The double pilasters which
farm the window piers are linked by
escutcheons. Above the windows are
masks set between convex and concave volutes; below the windows are
busts surrounded by volutes, resulting
in an extremely decorative façade.

124 centre ■

Herengracht 170-172
Hendrick de Keyser
1617 Huis Bartolotti

This large, rich house stands on a
bend in the canal, which is expressed
in the façade. The top part of the
façade is a stepped gable with stringcourses which are interrupted here
and there, balustrades and tapered
pilasters. Note the triglyph decoration
which has piping instead of the usual
grooves. The building is now used by
the Hendrick de Keyser Association.

125 centre ☐

Nieuwebrugsteeg 13/
St. Olofspoort
1618 In de Lompen

Renaissance stepped gable in
the manner of Lieven de Key. The
façade is subdivided by stone bands
which correspond to the sills of the
cross-windows. The frames are set
in semicircular arched niches whose
keystones are carved with heads of
humans and lions. A good example
of an early 17th century shop with
dwelling.

126 centre ☐

Muntplein
Hendrick de Keyser
1619 Munttoren

Originally formed part of the
Regulierspoort of 1490. The brick
base is partly round and partly poly-
gonal and becomes octagonal higher
up. Above this are four aediculae
with segmental pediments on which
the clock faces rest. The octagonal
lantern is entirely of timber dressed
with lead and with an openwork orb.
Coins were minted here in 1672 and
1673.

127 centre ■

Nieuwezijds Kolk
1620 Korenmetershuisje

There was already a corn measurers'
house here in 1558. In 1620 it was
replaced by a simple, rectangular
building with basement, main floor
and roof. Elevations with niches containing cross-windows. On the south
side above the entrance is a stone
tablet depicting the corn measurers'
attributes. Now the offices of the
Bond Heemschut.

128 centre ☐

Noordermarkt 44-48
Hendrick de Keyser
1620 Noorderkerk

Hendrick de Keyser's last church.
It had a modern plan for its time:
a Greek cross with small triangular
additions between its arms. The
façades are very simple and austere
and are slightly reminiscent of neck-
gables. Because they are lower than
the ridge of the main church the four
gables have been given hipped roofs.

129 centre ☐

Prinsengracht 279
Hendrick de Keyser
1620 Westerkerk

A fine renaissance church which is a
development of the earlier Zuiderkerk.
The 85 metres high spire is made up
of decreasing cube like sections and
is topped by the imperial crown from
the Amsterdam coat of arms. There
is still a gateway to the churchyard
adjoining the tower. Rembrandt's
grave is situated in the interior.

130 centre ☐

Keizersgracht 123
Pieter de Keyser
1622 Huis met de Hoofden

One of the largest double houses of
the period. The piers between the
windows are wide Doric pilasters
(with carvings of, from left to right,
Apollo, Ceres, Mars, Pallas Athena,
Bacchus and Diana) which are
extended upwards as double pilasters. Stepped gable with balustrades,
niches and a curved pediment.

131 centre ■

Keizersgracht 177
Jacob van Campen
1624 Coymanshuizen

Double house with a façade in the
style of Palladio and Scamozzi, with
pilasters and heavy cornices. At the
lower level the pilasters are Ionic and
above Composite. Note the absence
of perrons, gable-end, balustrading
and playful decoration, resulting in
a taut, austere elevation.

132 centre ■

Nieuwendijk 30
1630

The vertical emphasis in this stepped gable is reinforced by the continuous niche which runs from the second floor to the round attic window. The two small windows in niches on each side of the attic window are elements which were to be used 15 years later in the classical pilaster façade.

133 centre ■

Singel 411/Spui
Pieter de Keyser (attrib.)
1633 Oude Lutherse Kerk

Appears from the outside to be a two-aisled church on an irregular site; on the inside a rectangular hall church. On three sides there are two tiers of galleries. The church has been repeatedly altered and restored. Now in use as the assembly hall of the University of Amsterdam.

134 centre □

Jodenbreestraat 4-6
Jacob van Campen
1633

1606 stepped gable changed in accordance with Scamozzi's book of orders. It was the first house in Amsterdam to be capped by a pediment. From 1639 to 1658 the house was occupied by Rembrandt and it now houses Museum Het Rembrandthuis.

135 centre □

Nieuwezijds Voorburgwal 75
1633 Makelaarscomptoir

Asymmetrical façade caused by the pointed site resulting from the traditional street pattern. Cross-windows with continuous stone bands, spring-stones, keystones and volutes. On the last step is a niche with a shell motif above which is a triangular pediment. The building is now used by the Dutch Garden Foundation.

136 centre ■

Sloterkade 21
1634 Aalsmeerder Veerhuis/
Bonte Os

This formerly isolated building consists of a hall, corresponding to the width of the wooden entrance front, with a stepped gable. Adjoining this are side rooms which are two window bays wide. Various organisations involved in restoration work are now accommodated here.

137 tram 1, 2 □

Brouwersgracht 188-194
1636 Koning David, David,
Groene & Grauwe Valk

Four warehouses with fine, simple spout-gables front and rear. The linked hatches in the middle are now glazed. The two adjacent windows also had shutters originally. They were good examples of 17th century functional building and have now been converted into apartments.

138 centre ■

Kromboomssloot 18-20
1636 Schottenburg

Fine example of warehouses from the
first half of the 17th century. The linking of the two warehouses gives rise
to asymmetrical gable ends. Simple
window-frames in niches with brick
arches. The hatches are linked verti-
cally. Now converted into apartments.

139 centre ■

Oudebrugsteeg 7/Beursstraat
Jacob van Campen (attrib.)
1638 Accijnshuis

A classical building with giant pilasters set on pedestals. The Ionic capitals support a straight cornice and
attic to which windows were added
at a later date. The old and new city
coats of arms can be seen in the
façade (Koggeschip and the three
crosses).

140 centre □

Herengracht 168
Philips Vingboons
1638 Witte Huis

Entire façade in white sandstone
with a step as a gable ending with
extremely austere scrolls and vases.
The client, Michel Pauw, Knight
of St. Mark, had the two lions of
St. Mark placed at the top as shield-
bearers. Fine 18th century interiors
by Jacob de Wit and J. de Moucheron.

141 centre ■

Keizersgracht 319
Philips Vingboons
1639

First example of Vingboons' use of
pilasters in the façade of a narrow
house. The two pairs of Doric pilasters support triangular pediments
above the second floor.
The top is decorated with pediments,
scrolls, garlands, vases and two oval
windows set in a waterleaf decoration.

142 centre ■

Staalstraat 7ab
Pieter de Keyser
1641 Saaihal

A trapezoid gable with draped sheets
which are also entwined around the
corner vases. The Amsterdam coat of
arms is set in a cartouche above the
tablet bearing the date. The façade
of this Drapers Hall is topped by the
imperial crown. The cross-windows
of the first floor have triangular pediments.

143 centre ■

's Gravenhekje 1 /
Prins Hendrikkade
Pieter de Keyser (attrib.)
1642

These four warehouses are united
by the two trapezium-shaped gables.
These gables, which are pierced by
oval and round attic windows, are in
turn linked by a pediment decorated
with festoons and a coat of arms
bearing the monogram of the West
Indische Compagnie.

144 centre ■

Bloemgracht 87-89-91
1642

A good example of traditional
'burgher' architecture. Three stepped
gables built on a minimal frontage
with timber lower fronts, cross-
windows in niches with elliptical
arches and tablets representing the
'townsman', the 'country-man' and
the 'seaman'. The stepped gables
are capped by corbelled pinnacles.
Restored in the 1940s by Jan de
Meijer.

145 centre ■

Oude Turfmarkt 145
Philips Vingboons
1642 House of P.J. Sweelinck

A pilaster façade with three tiers of
pilasters: the Tuscan, Ionic and Doric
orders on a rusticated base. The
façade of this building, originally one
half of a twin property, is given an
extra vertical emphasis by the reces-
sing of the cornice in the middle bay.
The rear part of the building is still
intact. The building is now part of the
university complex.

146 centre ■

Dam
Jacob van Campen
1648 Stadhuis van Amsterdam

Sometimes called the eighth wonder
of the world. A large building built
around two courtyards between which
are the grand hall. On a base two
orders of pilasters support minutely
carved cornices. The central pavilions
have pediments with allegorical
carvings by Quellien, who was also
responsible for much of the interior
sculpture. The town hall is now used
as a Royal Palace and museum.

147 centre ☐

Palmgracht 28-38
1648 Rapenhofje

Almshouses founded by Pieter
Adriaensz. Raep for elderly women
and orphans belonging to the
Reformed Church. On the street
side it is a modest building with an
entrance gate, a coat of arms and
a barred cross window. Entrance by
a simple door which can be opened
fully or partly. Around the courtyard
is a row of houses which still have
their original cross-windows.

148 centre ☐

Karthuizerstraat 21-127
Daniel Stalpaert
1650 Nieuwezijds
Huiszitten-weduwenhof

This complex consists of the earliest type of dwelling: the one-roomed house. The simple façade has a central pavilion with pediment and two side-pavilions. The gutter board forms a low cornice. The striking lintels above the windows are in carefully rubbed red bricks. In the courtyard the pediments display the Amsterdam coat of arms.

149 centre ☐

Singel 83-85
1652 Veerhuis De Swaen

The front and side elevations, which both lean forward, have pilasters with Ionic capitals bearing a continuous cornice. Under the windows are festoons and date plaques. The lowest festoon of the middle bay has a hanging cloth rather than fruit.

150 centre ☐

Oudezijds Voorburgwal 316
Philips Vingboons
1655 Ladder Jacobs

The central element with its Doric
and Ionic pilasters supports a straight
cornice and a pediment with an
'oeil-de-boeuf', festoons and swags.
On the second floor the fruit festoons
become swags at the supports.
The stone tablet shows a pilgrim
at rest and two angels.

151 centre ■

Kattenburgerplein 1
Daniel Stalpaert
1655 's Lands Zeemagazijn

A sturdy, square storehouse with
projecting pavilions in the middle
and on the sides. One of the pediments, all of which were designed
by Quellien, represents the Admiralty
with sea deities and cannon.
Another depicts Neptune and
Amphitrite. Now houses the
Nederlands Scheepvaartmuseum
(Navigation Museum).

152 centre ☐

Keizersgracht 214
1656

A pilaster façade with giant Ionic order on the first and second storeys and entablatures in the outer bays only. The attic floor has a raised neck-gable with Corinthian pilasters and round windows with moulded surrounds. Built in the style of Philips Vingboons.

153 centre ■

Zandhoek 2-7
Second half of the 17th century

A terrace of quaint, modest houses from the second half of the 17th century. They all have a high lower front concealing two storeys. The remaining storeys are more obviously expressed.

154 centre ■

Herengracht 364-370
Philips Vingboons
1662 Cromhouthuizen

Four façades entirely in sandstone,
built for Jacob Cromhout. Each has
a central element, festoons, window
pediments and oeil-de-boeufs. The
first two buildings are clearly wider
than the last two. Nr. 366, in which
the Bible Museum is now located,
has interiors by Jacob de Wit.

155 centre ☐

Singel 460
Philips Vingboons
1662 Odeon

Built on the site of the former brew-
ery 'Het Lam' as a residence for the
merchant Marselius. It has a raised
neck-gable and festoons under the
windows. The scrolls have been given
pinnacles. A cartouche surrounds the
hoisting-beam. One of the rooms at
the back of the building has a fine
19th century interior (see 304).

156 centre ☐

Kloveniersburgwal 29
Justus Vingboons
1662 Trippenhuis

The composition is determined by
eight giant Corinthian pilasters.
The central pavilion supports the
pediment which was richly decorated
by Jan Gijselingh de Oude. The
second and sixth bays, in which the
entrances are situated, are wider
and more richly decorated. The frieze
is decorated with putty and arabesques. Note the chimneys made to
look like cannons – the client was an
arms merchant.

157 centre ■

Oudezijds Voorburgwal 40
1663 Schuilkerk Het Haentje

Simple but well-proportioned spout-
gable standing on a timber lower
front. The secret church, also known
as 'Ons' Lieve Heer op Solder' and
dedicated to St. Nicolaas, is on the
top floor. The mid-18th century altar
depicts the baptism of Christ. Now
Museum Amstelkring, Ons' Lieve Heer
op Solder. The interior was renovated
recently by Frederik Franken.

158 centre □

Oudezijds Voorburgwal 187
1663

This merchant's house has a raised neck-gable with Corinthian pilasters and scrolls with carvings of Africans and Indians, reclining on bales of tobacco. As is often the case, this raised neck-gable has circular windows set in cartouches. The middle element with Ionic pilasters has fine festoons.

159 centre ■

Singel 11/Kattegat 2
Adriaan Dortsman
1668-1671 Ronde Lutherse Kerk

This round, domed church which has an ambulatory on half its circumference was burnt to the ground in 1822 in a fire caused by careless plumbers. Rebuilt in 1823 by T.F. Suys and J. de Greef, who gave it a coffered vault instead of the smooth vault with ribs.

160 centre ☐

Wittenburgergracht 25
Daniel Stalpaert
1669 Oosterkerk

Plan in the shape of a Greek cross in which the space between the arms has been partially filled by lower volumes. On the canal side is the main entrance whose elevation has a balustrade. The cornice of the lower volumes follows the relief of the walls whereas the cornice of the Greek cross strictly follows the plan without acknowledging the indentations of the wall.

161 centre ☐

3e Weteringdwarsstraat 33
Philips Vingboons
1670 Wevershuisje

One of the four hundred weavers' houses built for the city of Amsterdam. The 'voorhuis' has a timber entrance front with a simple staircase. Large, simple windows determine the elevation which is closed by a low cornice serving as a gutter. A good example of social housing in the 17th century. In 2008 the buildings were affected by subsidence caused by construction work for the North-South metro line.

162 centre ■

Nieuwe Amstelstraat 1-3
Elias Bouman
1670 Hoog Duitse Synagoge

This synagogue has austere elevations which are closed by a low cornice. The tripartite division of the elevations is achieved by the pilasters. The central part of the front elevation has a simple pediment on a slightly projecting cornice. The building is converted into Joods Historisch Museum (Jewish Historical Museum), by A. Cahen and Premsela Vonk, 1987.

163 centre ☐

Amstel 216
Adriaan Dortsman
1671 Gijsbert Dommer Huis

A flat façade with strongly banded stone window piers. Above the entrance is a balcony with a simple window surround. Above the frieze with its triglyphs is an attic in the form of a balustrade with its central part hollowed out to accommodate the leaf-shaped coat of arms.

164 centre ■

Keizersgracht 672-674
Adriaan Dortsman
1671 Museum Van Loon

Flat stone elevations with single
pilasters on the corners. The entrance
is emphasized by the balcony and
a concave section of the blind balustrade. The façade is closed by
a triglyph-frieze above which is a
partly open and partly blind balustrade with the characteristic 'bottle-
shaped' balusters. There are statues
on the balustrade.

165 centre ☐

St. Antoniesbreestraat 69
Elias Bouman
1671 Pintohuis

The façade is given a strong vertical
emphasis by the superimposition
of the buttresses on the wall piers.
The cornice, which echoes each
indentation in the façade, carries a
blind balustrade to conceal the roof.

166 centre ☐

Oudezijds Achterburgwal 201/
Rusland
1673

A slender raised neck-gable divided by pilasters. The two outermost pilasters have Ionic capitals and the two innermost have Corinthian capitals which bear a segmental pediment decorated with a shell motif. The stone tablet depicts a cooper.

167 centre ■

Mr. Visserplein 1-3
Elias Bouman
1675 Portugees Israëlitische
Synagoge

The low buildings around the synagogue enclose a courtyard. The front elevation is subdivided by pilasters, the ones at the corners standing slightly free of the corner itself. The austere elevations with the corner bays slightly recessed are closed by a cornice above which is a balustrade and attic.

168 centre ☐

Herengracht 394/Leidsegracht
Last quarter of the 17th
century - Vier Heemskinderen

This little house has a neck-gable with a segmental pediment. Fine façade tablet depicting 'the four Heemskinderen' on their horse Beyaart (characters from a medieval legend). There are simple festoons under the windows and around the hoisting beam.

169 centre ■

Amstel 51
Hans Petersom
1681-1683 Diaconie Oude Mannen-
en Vrouwenhuis

With its 31 bays this was the widest building in the city. The main entrance with Ionic pilasters is situated in the middle five bays which carry a simple pediment. The two side entrances have Doric pilasters. The austere character of the elevational treatment can best be seen in the façades of the inner courtyard. The 'Hermitage on the Amstel', an Amsterdam branch of St. Petersburg's Hermitage Museum was opened here in 2009.

170 centre □

Prinsengracht 857-897
Pieter Adolfse de Zeeuw
1695 Deutzenhofje

These almshouses were for destitute
women of the Reformed faith. The
entrance has simple stone pilasters
and an almost 18th century cornice
with two putti. A stone tablet records
the foundation date. The trustees'
room above the entrance is decorated festoons and the family coats
of arms of the clients.

171 centre ■

Kloveniersburgwal 26
1696 Klein Trippenhuis

This small sandstone façade is only
one bay wide (2.5 metres). The low
cornice, which is raised in the centre
to a semi-circle, carries two sphinxes.
The frieze has festoons and an hour
glass.

172 centre ■

Eighteenth century

The seventeenth century was a period in which architecture, like the economy, was thriving. During the eighteenth century prosperity was maintained, but the gap widened between the rich and the poor. The population as a whole hardly increased. There was, therefore, little demand for new housing development. Nevertheless, building activity did not altogether cease. Many older, often seventeenth centuries, houses were rebuilt. They were provided with a new façade or even an entirely different interior. Most of the canal houses dated as eighteenth century have, in fact, a similar older core.

The country houses of rich Amsterdammers are often conversions of older property. Only Frankendaal still remains of the numerous estates in the Watergraafsmeer. Along the Amstel, Amstelrust and Oostermeer are still in existence.

This period of greater poverty among the people created the need for better ser-vices for the poor. Several new 'hofjes' (almshouses) were founded, of which Corvershof and the Van Brants-Rushofje is the most important from the architectural point of view.

The Louis Styles

Around 1700 the Amsterdam street scene was very varied on account of the great variety of gable types. For the rest of the eighteenth century too, gable endings, such as the neck-gable and bell-gable, remained common for the smaller private house. These gables are suitable for concealing the roof, which is at a right angle to the street. The eighteenth century neck-gables and bell-gables are often higher than those of the century before. The decorated stone scrolls are embellished in the various Louis styles, which, in imitation of France, became fashionable in the course of the century.

In the first part of the century, the Louis XIV style with its somewhat heavy, baroque shapes was adopted especially on the neck-gables. The often asymmetrical rococo shapes of the Louis XV style, which was used in the third quarter of the century, were not very suitable for the rectangular neck-gable. The bell-gable was now preferred. The strong and regular Louis XVI style of about 1780 was not often seen in conjunction with gable ends. Prinsenstraat 12 is the only neck-gable of that period. Numerous simpler types existed alongside the richly worked neck-gables and bell-gables. The neck-gable was marketed as an 'of-the-peg' article, which sometimes caused problems with adaptation to the plot width. This then led to the addition of, for example, vases on the corners.

The straight cornice was considered more suitable for wider houses with more than three bays and in which the ridge of the roof was parallel to the street. Many seventeenth century houses were provided with such a cornice and attic during the eighteenth century. Herengracht 476 is a fine example of this. In the seventeenth century the cornice served mainly as a gutter for the drainage of rainwater. In the course of the eighteenth century it was also given a clear architectural significance. The cornice, applied with great freedom and refinement together with an attic often formed the crowning glory of the façade. The attic was often entirely or partly worked open as a balustrade, above which statues and other ornaments were sometimes placed. These decorations were similar to the gable ends in the different Louis styles. The Regency style, which developed as a transitional form between the Louis XIV and Louis XV styles in France, was only followed to a slight extent in Amsterdam around 1725. Huize van Brienen at Herengracht 284 is an exceptional example of this. If a straight cornice instead of a gable end was demanded for a building less than three bays wide, the cornice itself or the attic was raised in the centre. This also served to hide the ridge or to enable a hatch to be made for easier use of the hoisting beam. Apart from the emphasis on the straight or raised cornice, the rather flat façades of the houses were characterized by the decorated central element. This middle bay was often emphasized by a double perron, a doorpost-framing and decorations around the middle window on the first floor. With richer houses these surrounds continued upwards to the cornice. There are many canal houses, especially from the Louis XIV period, which are decorated in such a way as to give the impression that they are palaces. The Grachtenboek of 1767 with drawings by Caspar Philips of almost 1500 houses is an important source for checking whether they are still in their original state.

The façades of the bigger houses are mostly of sandstone, and cheaper brick is used for the simpler neck-gables and bell-gables, although Abraham van der Hart did use brick for his Armenhuis and Maagdenhuis around 1780. These were, however, commissions in which great simplicity was aimed at. Towards the end of the century the brick front was often plastered, creating a smooth, monumental effect.

The window, which in the eighteenth century was to become an important compositional element in the façades, had been designed since the Middle Ages as a cross made up of a mullion and transom. However, after 1710 the French sliding sash window made its entrance. The division of the window changed in the course of the century. Most houses were given windows with bigger window-panes.

The interior became lighter through the use of the tall sash window and through the increasing use of stucco ceilings. The interior, in contrast to the seventeenth century, was designed more as a unity. The rooms were no longer regarded as being separated from each other. The hall and the staircase were given a central place.

Daniel Marot

The enormous influence of the French building styles, clearly visible in the interiors, reached Amsterdam mainly through Daniel Marot, who lived here from 1705 till 1717. In the following years the undeniable influence of his Louis XIV style can be seen in the stucco and façade designs such as those of the decorator-architects Jan van Logteren and Frans Blanchard. In the forties the fairly heavy baroque shapes of Marot were used in a more playful way by the brothers Hans Jacob and Hendrick Husly.

In the eighteenth century there was no clear leader among the architects. However, Jacob Otten Husly, the cousin of the brothers Husly mentioned above, played an important role after 1750. His design for Felix Meritis in 1788 with its Corinthian half columns was an exceptional building for Amsterdam. During the Louis periods in Amsterdam, pillars or pilasters, along the entire façade, were hardly used, in contrast to France. This changed around 1770. Herengracht 527 is a very early example of this. This return to classical motifs, known in France as the Louis XVI style, had little influence in Amsterdam and only led to a tightening of the design language. Thus, the Armenhuis and the Maagdenhuis were built in a restrained, simple style by Abraham van der Hart, city architect in the last quarter of the century. The only decorations were to be found in the pediments, by Anthonie Ziesenis, the most important sculptor of that period.

Middenweg 72
1st quarter 18th century
Frankendael

This country house consists of a main building flanked by a stable and a coach house. The brickwork front elevation has a timber cornice and balustrade. The garden has a fountain by Ignatius van Logteren (1714) and an entrance gate (1783) with the coat of arms of J. Gildemeester (see parks).

201 tram 9 ☐ (gardens only)

Kromboomsloot 22
1714 Heilige Geest

After a hundred years as a Roman Catholic Church the building was re-purchased by the Armenian community in 1986 and restored. The doorway with an Armenian text and a carving of a lamb and the steps are noteworthy.

202 centre ■

Herengracht 554
1716

The original 17th century house was rebuilt in 1716 and was given an attic and two statues on the straight cornice. The centre is emphasized by a richly decorated balcony and the double perron – both added as part of the restoration.

203 centre ■

Herengracht 539
Jean Coulon (attrib.)
1718

This property was altered in 1718 by G. Corver, probably after an original design for Herengracht 433 by Coulon. The monumental sandstone façade is only three bays wide and has a balcony supported by female figures and, above the cornice, a blind attic with a raised central section and statues.

204 centre ■

1e Weteringdwarsstraat 11-43
1721-1731 Grill's Hofje

These pleasant almshouses for
elderly women have nine identical
bell-gables on the street side. Pairs
of houses share a common timber
entrance stair. The street at the rear
is reached through the middle house
(nr. 19) and has six more houses
and a clock of 1727. There is also
a trustees' room.

205 centre ☐

Kloveniersburgwal 6-8
1722 Abraham and Isaac

Formerly number 4 had a similar
neck-gable with a carving of Jacob
at the top. Now Isaac (nr. 8) alone
looks at patriarch Abraham (nr. 6)
who stares straight ahead. These two
properties with their common timber
front and separate single-bay brickwork façades were restored in 1980.

206 centre ■

Nieuwe Herengracht 6-18
1723 Corvershof

Almshouses founded by J. Corver and
S. Trip for poverty-stricken elderly
couples, now part of the Amstelhof.
The central element in the façade,
bounded by two Ionic pilasters, is
closed by a segmental pediment in
which an allegory of charity is accompanied by an eagle bearing the coat
of arms of the 'hof'.

207 centre ■

Keizersgracht 444-446
1725

This richly decorated baroque façade
does not look very Dutch. The two
properties were combined in 1758
and were altered several times. The
rendered sandstone elevation ends
with a cornice with attic and centrepiece. Unfortunately, the original
double entrance perron has been
removed.

208 centre ■

Lange Leidsedwarsstraat 129-131
1726

Double neck-gable with unusual scrolls (volutes) with an acanthus motif, under which is a tablet depicting a cow's head and the year.
The property on the left is still in its original condition. Four bell-gables on nrs. 148-154 were built fifty years later.

209 centre ■

Herengracht 520
1726-1727

This property was completely altered. A façade with cornice, attic and alliance coats of arms was added as well as decorated windows and a door with Ionic pilasters and curved architrave. The original window divisions have been removed. The entrance stair with its mouldings and railings is particularly fine.

210 centre ■

Prins Hendrikkade 133
1727

Residence in the Louis XIV style with sandstone facing and richly decorated cornice and attic. The cornice has an arched central section flanked by tritons blowing horns, a Mercury staff and two corner vases. Only the centre window on the first floor has a decorated surround.

211 centre ■

Diemerzeedijk 27
Cornelis van der Hoeven
1727 Gemeenlandshuis

A restored, plain, dignified building with corner pilasters on a simple façade. The entrance was originally more richly decorated. The interior has carvings by Pierre le Normant and plasterwork by Christiaan Wittenbeeker. Now Hoogheemraadschap Amstelland (polder authority).

212 tram 3, 26 □

Herengracht 284
1728 Huize Van Brienen

Originally built in the 17th century, this property was rebuilt in the Regency style in 1728. It came into possession of the Van Brienen family in 1781. Since 1932 it has been owned by the Hendrick de Keyser Society, an organization which is responsible for the purchase and restoration of many properties. Sandstone façade with a straight cornice, attic and frieze with small windows. The interior and the summer-house are well worth viewing.

213 centre ☐ (on request)

Keizersgracht 606-608
1730

Two neck-gables in the Louis XIV style. Among the largest in Amsterdam. Nr. 610 had an identical façade until 1790. The gables are capped by crests. The hoisting-beam opening is decorated. Nr. 606 has an early 19th century door and a bench on the perron.

214 centre ■

Herengracht 475
Hans Jacob Husly (attrib.)
1730

House with monumental sandstone
façade in Louis XIV style with a fine
doorpost-framing and two female
figures on the first floor. The façade
is closed by a straight cornice with
attic and balustrade. The house has
a splendid interior in which the hall
and staircase occupy a prominent
position with important plasterwork
and sculpture.

215 centre ☐ (on request)

Nieuwe Keizersgracht 28-44
Daniel Marot
1732 Van Brants-Rushofje

Almshouses founded by Chr. van
Brants for Evangelical Lutheran
women. The brick façade with its
decorated centre element and
double stairs has a relief depicting
Charity above the cornice. Above the
entrance is a eulogy to the founder.
The 'hofje' has a fine trustees' room.

216 centre ■

Herengracht 495
Jean Coulon
1739

Original 17th century façade rebuilt
for Jan Six. The balcony with its
wrought-iron railings and the text
Omnia orta occidunt dates from
1775. The stone façade is closed
by a cornice, attic and balustrade.

217 centre ■

Oudezijds Voorburgwal 215-217
2nd quarter 18th century

The façade has a blind attic, richly
embellished in the centre above a
straight cornice. The form of the
balustrade is especially interesting. The illusion of curving inwards
above the outer bays is caused by
the downward bending. The cornice
has decorated consoles and hoisting
beams. There are small windows in
the frieze.

218 centre ■

Herengracht 164
1750-1775

Four-bay façade with a straight cornice and attic. Above the attic, which is treated as a balustrade and centrepiece, are four vases. The doorpost-framing with its Ionic pilasters is original.

219 centre ■

Nieuwe Herengracht 143
1750

The bluestone façade has a raised cornice in which an attic window has been placed. Below the cornice are plain consoles and rectangles. The door and window mouldings are in comparatively low relief. The elevation is bounded by banded corner pilasters.

220 centre ■

Nieuwe Herengracht 103
1751

This originally 17th century property
has a particularly fine entranceway
with sophisticated ironwork railings
to the steps and a rococo doorpost-
framing. The bluestone façade is
closed by cornices under which are
fanciful consoles. On the first floor is
a fine room with a double fireplace.

221 centre ■

Jonas Daniel Meijerplein
G.F. Maybaum
1752 Nieuwe Synagoge

This austere, symmetrical building
has a balustrade with a semicircular
centrepiece above the cornice and
a small dome on the roof. The
entrance has imbedded Ionic columns. The building was closed
in 1936 but has now been restored
(A, Cahen/Premsela Vonk) and since
1987 has become, together with
the adjoining synagogue, the Joods
Historisch Museum (Jewish Historical
Museum).

222 centre □

Herengracht 39
1753 Gouda

In the 18th century warehouses were usually much simpler than their predecessors. This property, however, has a richly decorated bell-gable. Nr. 37 is again much plainer. Both have unusual, timber lower fronts. This indicates a combined function as a storage and office space.

223 centre ■

Kloveniersburgwal 72
Pieter Rendorp
1754 Oudemanhuis

These former almshouses for elderly men and women have belonged to Amsterdam University since 1876. There are four wings enclosing an almost square courtyard. The elevations to this courtyard are in brickwork with stone porticos capped by triangular pediments. The city's coat of arms is displayed on the north pediment.

224 centre □ (access via 242)

Keizersgracht 546
1760

A good example of a Louis XV bell-gable with playful rococo volutes and a wide crest. The third floor still has its hoisting hatch. The window division is early 19th century. Little else has been altered.

225 centre ■

Roomolenstraat 11
1760

This property is unusual in that it is a neck-gable in Louis XV style. Usually the bell-gable was used for this playful ornamentation as the neck-gable was less suitable.

226 centre ■

Keizersgracht 224
1765 Saxenburg

Sandstone façade with four bays,
closed by a straight cornice and attic
with raised centre and decorative
vases. There is a double entrance
perron and the door and first floor
window have moulded surrounds.
The interior still has its 18th century
hall and staircase and a room with
plasterwork.

227 centre ☐

Prinsengracht 300
1767 't Vosje

This house, which was restored in
1959, received its name from the
17th century furrier's house on the
same site called De Witte Vos. Above
the two doors in the timber lower
front is a red fox with a bird in its
mouth. Below the hoisting beam
at the top of this fine bell-gable is
another fox.

228 centre ■

Herengracht 493
1770

The austere façade of this originally 17th century house is a good example of the late Louis XV style. The plasterwork in the interior dates from the 18th century. The sandstone façade with its pediment and attic has had its original window divisions restored.

229 centre ■

Herengracht 527
1770

Extremely early example of a Louis XVI façade with Ionic pilasters over the first and second storeys and a pediment with an eagle. Only the tall, hipped roof remains of the original 17th century house. The windows were altered around 1800.

230 centre ■

Alexanderplein
Cornelis Rauws
1770 Muiderpoort

Formerly one of the city gates.
A classical building with a central
dome and lantern. Above Doric columns the pediment has a relief carving of the Amsterdam coat of arms
by A. Ziesenis.

231 centre □

Nieuwe Keizersgracht 120
Coenraad Hoeneker
1771 Luthers Diaconiehuis

Restrained, dignified building almost
without decoration, apart from the
pediment with its clock. J. Otten
Husly probably participated in the
building operations. It is now the
Luthers Verpleeghuis (Lutheran
Nursing Home), which is inscribed
above the door. There is a fine trustees' room.

232 centre ■

Herengracht 182
Ludwig Friedrich Druck
1772 Zonnewijser

The name Sundial and the sun on the
façade are derived from the original
house. The house was built for Van
Brienen and has a sandstone façade
with straight cornice and attic. The
interior has plasterwork ceilings dating from 1772. The double entrance
perron was reconstructed during
the restoration of 1972. The house
is sometimes known as Huize Van
Brienen II (see 213).

233 centre ■

Nieuwe Keizersgracht 94
1774 Occo's Hof/Gesticht van
Barmhartigheid

The pediment above the stone portico of this austere Louis XVI façade,
displays the coat of arms of the
founder, C.E. Occo. The 'hofje', form-
ally for poor widows and spinsters
has a trustees' room and a fine
garden court. It was extended and
modernized in the 19th century when
the chapel was also demolished.

234 centre ■

Geldersekade 8
1775 Tabaksvat

Louis XVI façade with austere, straight cornice. There are garlands between the consoles and an attic window in the centre. The frieze is higher than usual to accommodate this attic window. Above the door is a relief showing two baskets and a cask and the text Tabaksvat (Tobacco cask).

235 centre ■

Prinsenstraat 12
c. 1775

An unusual house in that it is the only surviving example of a Louis XVI neck-gable in Amsterdam. On the top is a carving of a beehive. There is now a shop in the 19th century lower front.

236 centre ■

Middenweg 4-6/Ringdijk
Caspar Philips
1777 Rechthuis

The Courthouse of the former independent district of Watergraafsmeer also served as an inn. This brick building has Doric columns next to the entrance and garlands around the middle window. The portico is crowned by a pediment and by a turret on the roof. The original steps and lanterns have been removed.

237 tram 9 ■

Roeterstraat 2
Abraham van der Hart
1779-1782 Armen Werkhuis

This present-day nursing home was designed as a home for criminals and the poor: both of which groups are depicted in the tympanum with the patroness of the city in a relief by A. Ziesenis. This dignified building with its almost complete lack of ornamentation has a classical feel about it. The building was praised for its light, air and hygiene and was imitated in the Maagdenhuis (see 240).

238 tram 7 ■

Vierwindendwarsstraat 1
1781 Drie Gekroonde Haringen

A house which is freestanding on three sides. The sloping roof-planes are carried round the three open sides. There is a straight cornice and corner chimneys which were reconstructed as part of the restorations. The original glazing bars have also been reinstalled, reinforcing the restrained dignity of this simple, brick building. The three crowned herrings are depicted in the doorpost-framing, which is also original.

239 tram 3 ■

Spui
Abraham van der Hart
1783-1787 Maagdenhuis

This accommodation for Roman Catholic orphaned girls was, like the Armen Werkhuis (238), to be 'free of pomp and adornment but sound and strong'. The interior of this brick building with its stone entrance and tympanum by A. Ziesenis has been altered and modernized. It has been owned by the University of Amsterdam since 1961.

240 centre □

Amstel 56
Abraham van der Hart
1785 Franse Schouwburg

This taut, austere building was formerly the French Theatre. A small
pediment above the dormer and the
straight cornice are the only ornaments. Van der Hart introduced a
new type of window from France. It
had larger panes than had previously
been usual. For a hundred years the
building has been occupied by the
Kleine Komedie Theatre.

241 centre ☐

Kloveniersburgwal
A. Ziesenis
1786 Oudemanhuispoort

The Oudemanhuispoort provides
access to the university building
and to a second-hand book market.
The sculpture by Ziesenis portrays
a maiden offering a cornucopia to
two aged figures. The gate on the
Oudezijds Achterburgwal (1754)
has an arched pediment with a pair
of spectacles symbolizing old age.

242 centre ☐

Keizersgracht 324
Jacob Otten Husly
1788 Felix Meritis

This imposing building with its four
sturdy imbedded columns was the
office of the Felix Meritis Fellowship,
the cultural centre of Amsterdam.
The decorations on the façade por-
tray the various arts. Inside is an oval
room which later served as the model
for the Kleine Zaal of the Concertgebouw (see 339). Most of the
building had to be rebuilt after the
fire of 1932.

243 centre ☐

Nieuwe Herengracht 20
1789-1790 Bestedelingenhuis/
Amstelrank

From the poem above the entrance
it would appear that the building
was paid for from the legacy of
Johanna van Mekeren-Bontekoning.
Completely freestanding, the building
is characterized by its great austerity
(both outside and inside), this in
contrast to the adjacent Corvershof
(see 207). It is now the Amstelhof's
staff residence.

244 centre ■

Singel 145
1790

Simple late 18th century bell-gable;
noteworthy for its unusual Louis XVI
decoration. The door is original.

245 centre ■

Herengracht 40
Jacob Otten Husly (attrib.)
1790-1791

Calm, distinguished building, constructed by T.A. van Iddekinge.
One of the few late 18th century
residential properties. The wide sandstone façade is closed by a straight
cornice with consoles and rosettes.
The semicircular fanlights on the
main floor are noteworthy.

246 centre ■

Kloveniersburgwal 50
Abraham van der Hart/
B.W.H. Ziesenis
1792-1793 Hersteld Evangelisch
Lutherse Gemeente

Only the classical façade of this
church, which has been disused
since 1950, is still intact. The relief
in the pediment is by A. Ziesenis,
whose son was also involved in the
construction of the building. The central pavilion with rusticated base has
six Ionic pilasters, carrying a cornice
and pediment.

247 centre ☐

Herengracht 502
Abraham van der Hart
1792 Deutzhuis

This originally 17th century house
was rebuilt by Abraham van der Hart
for C. Deutz van Assendelft. The
emphasis in the severe façade with
its straight cornice is on the central
entrance whose two Doric columns
support the marble balcony. There
is still a room in the Louis XVI style.
Official residence of the mayor since
1927.

248 centre ■

Nineteenth century

In the nineteenth century as in the eighteenth century Dutch architects mainly followed developments abroad. Nineteenth century Amsterdam can be approached in two different ways: as an isolated period, with its jumble of styles and strange, new building commissions such as stations, circuses and industrial palaces, or as a period in which specifically after about 1860 the foundations of the period 1900-1940 are laid, the period in which Dutch architecture played a leading role for a short while. For a foreigner the second approach is perhaps more interesting than the first one, for, generally speaking, he will search in vain for the spectacle that nineteenth century towns like Paris, Vienna, Brussels and London have to offer. The post – 1895 economic revival – hesitant in the sixties, then strong again after 1875 and again after a crisis towards the end of the eighties, came too late for this. It is not possible to detect a similar sharp split between the first and the second half in most European capitals. The development of Amsterdam had stagnated until 1860. There was no population growth, no migration and hardly any movement in the social structure. There were hardly any economic developments. From 1830 onwards advantage was taken of the profits, yielded by the so-called forced farming system (Cultuur stelsel) on Java. More buildings were demolished than built. The gable ends of houses were truncated by the hundred and, in the interest of cheapness as well as under the influence of 'classicism', they were provided with extremely simple straight cornices.

Louis Napoleon

One can hardly speak of architecture under these circumstances. It is true that, during the French occupation, King Louis Napoleon, the man who turned the town hall into the Koninklijk Paleis (Royal Palace), did as much as possible for the arts and especially for architecture. He enabled young architects to study on a grant in Paris and Rome. In their few large projects, these 'pensionnaires' (Suys, Zocher, De Greef) were in fact the only architects to show any affinity with international developments from the 1820's onwards. From sheer necessity all superfluous decoration was left out in their work. As all religious denominations had had freedom of worship since the French period, a number of churches were also built during this period. However, production was still low in this field in comparison with the second half of the century when, especially since the rehabilitation of the Episcopal hierarchy in the Roman-Catholic church (1853), the silhouette of Amsterdam was enriched with a great number of church towers. From the fifties onwards a modest impulse was also given to building activity by so-called philanthropical working-class housing. This attempted to improve the appalling living conditions in the Jordaan and other working-class areas, which were considered a danger to public health, by building large estates, amply provided with light and air.

Paleis voor Volksvlijt

Foreign travellers visiting Amsterdam in the 1860's and 1870's were surprised at the apathy and phlegmatism with which the city allowed itself to be surpassed by other capitals and by various industrial' boom-towns'. The upturn was symbolized by the Paleis voor Volksvlijt (1857-1864, destroyed by fire 1929), one of the strangest glass and iron industrial palaces that Europe has seen. Inspired by the Crystal Palace of the Great Exhibition of 1851, it was the brainchild of Dr. Samuel Sarphati who is known as 'the founder of modern Amsterdam'. Most of the large building projects in the second half of the nineteenth century, the period of flourishing liberal citizenship, were the results of the efforts of individuals or private companies: Artis Zoo, Vondelpark, Westergasfabriek, Stadsschouwburg etc. The architect of the Paleis voor Volksvlijt, which was crowned with a dome, and of the stately, still existing Amstel Hotel, was C. Outshoorn. He is considered the first modern architect who introduced an office system for his enterprise, like the en-gineers had already done before him. Partly self-taught and partly educated by a railway engineer, his special virtue was that he introduced a liberal scale of building and design to the Amsterdam of that period. With a sidelong glance at the French 'modern renaissance', as the architecture of the Second Empire was known, his work showed an eclecticism which was somewhat lacking in direction.

P.J.H. Cuypers

P.J.H. Cuypers also derived his inspiration for the most part from France, albeit from the radical camp of Viollet-le-Duc. When he started, in 1876, with the designs for the Centraal Station and the Rijksmuseum, both in what he himself understood to be in a national style, for a quarter of a century he had been gaining experience in the building of several Catholic churches in the south of the Netherlands, most of them in Romanesque or early-Gothic style. Cuypers was regarded by many architects of the first part of the twentieth century as the grandfather of modern building (Berlage, of course, being the father) because he re-thought the basic principles of architecture, with the phrase he borrowed from Viollet-le-Duc as a motto above his work: 'toute forme qui n'est pas indiquée par la structure doit être repoussée' (all form which is not indicated by structure must be repulsed). Much of what took place in the period of 1900-1940 in Dutch architecture is hardly conceivable without the work of Cuypers; not only because of the emphasis on structural rationalism borrowed from Gothic church-building, but also because of his concept of a Gesamtkunstwerk which, from ground plan and structure to the tiniest detail should be governed by one regulating principle. There is an almost straight line linking the Rijksmuseum to Berlage's Koopmansbeurs (1898-1903). It is striking that both buildings tell an elaborate story - the one about Dutch (art) history, the other about the history of Amsterdam as a merchant city. Both architects were advised by sympathising men of letters. And, in addition, both followed the architecture and the iconography of the Stadhuis on the Dam.

Dutch neo-Renaissance

Neo-Renaissance too, participated in the revival of architecture in the late nine-teenth century. The Maatschappij ter Bevordering der Bouwkunst (Dutch Society of Architects, founded in 1842) supported eclecticism as the more or less offi-cial line after 1850. From this the Dutch neo-Renaissance developed slowly but gradually. In the 1880's and 1890's it was the dominant school of architecture. As early as the 1860's I. Gosschalk (a pupil of Gottfried Semper), was an advo-cate of this style. He pleaded against the diluted carpenter's classicism, against Cuyper's neo-Gothic style and against the eclectic styles of the Maatschappij. Like Cuypers his point of departure was the indigenous Dutch brick style of the sixteenth and early seventeenth century. Next to the Maatschappij a more artistic unrestrained society existed, called Architectura et Amicitia. The central figure was Jan L. Springer. He was a bohemian, more renowned for his French-style sketches and admired by the younger neo-Renaissance architects for his terrific architectural fantasies. Ed. Cuypers (a pupil of his uncle P.J.H. Cuypers) provided the link between the late nineteenth century and the more individual expressionism of the Amsterdam School architecture. Just before the turn of the century he abandoned neo-Renaissance. Through his work several important influences reached Dutch architecture, especially those of Norman Shaw and the modern English country-house style (which was also noticeable in the work of A. Salm). In 1899 Ed. Cuypers took on the fifteen-year-old Michel de Klerk in his new studio in the Jan Luykenstraat. De Klerk left in 1910 when his style had already been shaped for the greater part.

Art Nouveau

Art Nouveau is almost entirely absent from Amsterdam with the exception of sev-eral tiled tableaux, shop fronts and insurance buildings. It was rejected as being too 'decorative'. The variant was the Nieuwe Kunst which was more adapted to the old Dutch virtues of truth and craftsmanship in construction. The American Hotel by W. Kromhout, a member of the influential, but in the 1890's still mainly theoretically active Architectura group, provided an interim climax. Within this group, Berlage was strongly influenced by some austerely designed competition entries by K.P.C. de Bazel. Neither were the developments in modern American architecture to remain unnoticed. The most important activities of Berlage, Kromhout and De Bazel, however, took place after the turn of the century.

Prinsengracht 436
J. de Greef
1825-1829 Paleis van Justitie

De Greef, city architect from 1820-
1834, rebuilt the Aalmoezeniers-
weeshuis (Almoners' Orphanage) as
a Court of Justice around two courtyards. The interior and the hall have
been well preserved. Semicircular
arches to the entrance as at the
Stadhuis on the Dam Square (147).
Sober classicism with pavilions
emphasized by pilasters and balustrades, Empire style windows.

301 centre ☐

Groenburgwal 42
J. Jansen (church)
1827-1829 English Episcopal
Church

Early example of Romantic Gothic on
one of the most picturesque canals.
Former Draper's Hall converted into
church in 1827. In 1829 the vicarage, in front of the actual church
and formerly the home of Hendrick
de Keyser, was given a new façade,
probably designed by an unknown
English architect. With its orange-
red brickwork it fits in well with its
surroundings. Until the 1860's neo-
Gothicism was purely decorative.

302 centre ■

Kadijksplein
J. de Greef/C.W.M. Klijn/
G. Moele
1827 Former Rijks-Entrepot

Viewed from the Plantage Doklaan
an impressive row of different warehouses, mostly 19th century. In 1857
51 existing warehouses were bought
by the State and partly rebuilt. Thirty-
three new warehouses were built
and onto Kadijksplein administrative
buildings were added in an austere
Doric style. The colonnade was later
bricked up. In the nineties the warehouses are converted into apartments
by J. van Stigt.

303 centre ☐ grounds only

Singel 460
M.G. Tétar van Elven
1837 Concertzaal Odeon

Despite restricted entry and the
paintwork, the concert hall on the
first floor is worth a visit. In the
1840's and 1850's. the classicist
Tétar van Elven dominated the architectural scene – although he had
few commissions. The parabolic
shape of the auditorium, intended to
give good acoustics, was calculated
by a teacher from the Jordaan.

304 centre ☐

Waterlooplein 205
T.F. Suys/J. van Straaten
1837-1841 St. Antonius van Padua/
Mozes en Aäronkerk

A classical building, originally built-in on both sides. Designed by the Fleming Suys (Prix de Rome, a pupil of Percier), and executed by Van Straaten. Finally it was built with three-quarter round pilasters, because of city regulations which forced the architect to reduce the portico. Wooden towers inspired by St. Sulpice in Paris. During restoration (1969) all the woodwork and sandstone was painted a sandstone colour.

305 centre ☐

Haarlemmerplein 50
C. Alewijn/C.W.M. Klijn
1840 Willemspoort

Neoclassical gatehouse for the assessment and collection of local taxes. Corinthian columns, not completely accurate as the masons misjudged the entasis; hence the overtapering under the astragal. Capitals by the sculptor De Koningh who also worked on those of the Madeleine in Paris. Restored and converted to dwellings in 1986.

306 centre ☐

Dam/Nieuwezijds Voorburgwal
M.G. Tétar van Elven
1844

Six monumental, bronze-coloured,
cast-iron lamp-posts, richly decorated
with acanthus leaves and winged
lions. Tétar van Elven is described as
a 'gifted man' who had little chanche
to develop his talents during this
period of low building activity.

307 centre ☐

Houtmanstraat 1-27/
Planciusstraat
P.J. Hamer
1854-1856 Modelwoningblok
Vereeniging ten
behoeve der
Arbeidersklasse

'Philantropic' housing for the working
classes (see 314). Equal window
heights and characteristic access
by way of centrally placed well-lit,
staircases. A large, subtly composed
block, especially on the Houtman-
straat: seven pavilions divided into
three types, attached in different
ways; window types vary according
to size of the dwelling unit.

308 tram 3 ■

Keizersgracht 676
A.N. Godefroy
1854-1856 Nieuwe Walenkerk/
Adventskerk

Hall church with galleries on cast-iron columns, with graceful lanterns. Sandstone façade complete with lanterns echoing the adjoining 17th century façades. Rusticated classical base below and round Romanesque arch style above. Lombardian arches moulding and heavy corner buttresses (altered in 1862 after fire). Godefroy was one of the major architects of (third-quarter) nineteenth century eclecticism.

309 centre ☐

Rokin 112
J.H. Leliman
1855 Arti et Amicitiae

An unorthodox building for its time, influenced by Leliman's teacher in Paris H. Labrouste. The rather restrained façade reflects a logical subdivision of the spaces behind: a blasphemy against the 'Beaux Arts' lessons of his (first) teacher M.G. Tétar van Elven. Sculpture by F. Stracké. Old Dutch staircase by H.P. Berlage/A.C. Bleys (1894). Houses an artists' society.

310 centre ☐ gallery & staircase

Keizersgracht 452
C. Outshoorn
1860 Woonhuis Fuld

17th century property, altered to a
classical residence with Baroque
decoration and heavy central
emphasis above the double perron.
Ornamentation in painted terracotta.
This is one of the last of a two-
hundred-year, unbroken tradition
of Italian and French influenced
stately canal houses, beginning with
Vingboons and Van Campen and
ending with Outshoorn.

311 centre ■

Haarlemmerstraat 126-128
P.J.H. Cuypers
1860-1863/1887-1889
Posthoornkerk

Gothic-Romanesque transept basilica
with cloverleaf choir, inspired by the
German Rhineland. The silhouette
makes it clear that Cuypers was
searching for a combination of a
basilica and a centralized church
early in his career. The two tiers of
galleries in the narrow interior, with
its subtle polychrome are noteworthy;
a reference to the original secret
church-building period. In 1989 the
interior was partly turned into offices
by A. van Stigt.

312 centre ■

Keizersgracht 609
C. Outshoorn
1861-1863 Museum FOAM

A conversion of 'Spook' warehouse
into a gallery for art collector
C.J. Fodor. Large room at rear with
skylight, now completely modernized.
Richly decorated façade in Bentheimer sandstone. Remarkably
narrow-looking windows. Now
houses the FOAM Fotografiemuseum
Amsterdam.

313 centre □

Westerstraat 195-215/327-405
Lijnbaansgracht 63-65
P.J. Hamer
1862-1864

Tenement blocks for 'philanthropic'
working-class housing societies
based on English precedents, often
initiated by businessmen influenced
by the Protestant Revival (Bible tract
on Lijnbaansgracht 64), with capital
retention and a low rate of interest.
Eclecticism: classical articulation with
pavilions and rusticated buttresses;
Romanesque and Gothic detailing.
Converted and restored in 1985.

314 centre ■

Prof. Tulpplein 1
C. Outshoorn
1863-1867 Amstel Hotel

Outshoorn succeeded here in giving the Amstel, together with the
Hogesluis (bridge), the metropolitan
allure, for which Sarphati had striven.
At a later date an extra storey was
added to the French Second Empire
wings, thus destroying the proportion
between the pavilions and the wings.

315 centre ☐

Amsteldijk 273
J.D. & L.P. Zocher
1869/1891-1892 Zorgvlied

The oldest section of the cemetery,
on the right-hand side, was landscaped in 1869 and has an open,
orderly arrangement. Carré (see 337)
the circus family's tomb (J.P.F. van
Rossem and W.J. Vuyk), the huge
'East Indian' Dorrepaal family grave
and the rather sentimental grave of
the banker Rosenthal are worth to
visit.

316 tram 25 ☐

Oude Turfmarkt 127
W.A. Froger
1865-1869 Nederlandse Bank

Designed as a conscious contrast to the National Bank in Brussels, which was considered too exuberant. Much attention was paid to the vertical accents in the pavilions, leading to a particularly successful balance. Curve in the building line echoed by rounded corners to the pavilion. Colour contrast in the façade achieved by the use of Bremer stone and Bentheimer stone. Now houses the Allard Pierson Museum of archaeology.

317 centre ☐

Plantage Lepellaan 6
W. & J.L. Springer
1874

Sumptuous and beautifully situated urban villa with garden in a quiet part of the Plantage. Mixture of renaissance and classicism. Red brickwork, Escauzine stone, sculptural ornamentation in reconstructed Portland cement bases stone. The bronze-painted statues and vases in the niches are zink: on the left a man with a sickle, on the right a woman holding her hands over a cooking pot. This suggests a possible winter and summer house.

318 tram 9 ■

Vondelstraat 73-75/77-79
P.J.H. Cuypers
1876/1881

77-79 – Double house with floor
plan symmetrically mirrored but with
a super-structure of two pitched
roofs at right angles to each other.
Architect Cuypers' former house
(nr. 77) has an altered entrance and,
on the left, some later additions.
Bracket under bay window derived
from Viollet-le-Duc, as is the rationalist planning. Sgrafitto tiled tableaux
showing: left, the architect, centre,
the mason and, on the right, the
jealous critic.

319 tram 1 ■

Vondelpark
J.D. & L.P. Zocher/J.J. Kerbert
1865-1877

By Amsterdam standards a large
open space. The oldest part by
J.D. Zocher has calm lines and
broad perspectives, in early English
landscape style. Pavilion, now Film
Museum (P.J. & W. Hamer, 1881).
Statue of the poet Vondel (L. Royer),
pedestal (P.J.H. Cuypers, 1867).
Monumental entrance railings on
the Stadhouderskade (A. Linneman,
1883). Round teahouse-functional-
ism (H.A.J. Baanders, 1937).

320 tram 1, 2, 5 □

Plantage Middenlaan 60
G.B. Salm
1878

In the Plantage there are many examples of 'carpenter's classicism' or 'plasterer's style' in which cheap and shoddy structures are hidden behind rendered façades: Salm, an architect who built soundly, shows that with good proportions and appropriate detailing even stuccoed architecture can please, in spite of a restricted budget.

321 tram 9 ■

Vossiusstraat 1-15
I. Gosschalk
1879

Succesful example of speculative building for the better-off. Fifteen terraced houses, in plan and section resembling an 18th century palace, incorporating two wings and pavilions. Louis XVI ornament with a meander, palmettos, Vitruvian Scroll, etc. Few vertical accents due to situation, immediately opposite Vondelpark.

322 tram 1, 2, 5 ■

Reguliersgracht 57-59/63
I. Gosschalk
1879/c. 1882

Two façades with a great deal of
carpentry. On the left the German
inspired façade with Old Dutch shop-
front which has been so well publi-
cised. The façade on the right
is more interesting, a combination
of Old Dutch with Old English and
Queen Anne. It is possible that
Gosschalk was acquainted with these
styles through the work of Norman
Shaw.

323 centre ■

Vondelstraat 120
P.J.H. Cuypers
1872-1880 Heilige Hartkerk/
Vondelkerk

Cuypers's masterpiece. Interior plun-
dered during vacancy (1979-1985).
The alterations and new function
make experience of interior difficult
but did make possible the preservation of the church. The church is
the centre of an oval square – also
designed by Cuypers. The building
combines an octagonal centralized
structure with a longitudinal axis.
The Gothic Liebfrauenkirche in Trier
and the Baroque church of Vierzehn-
heiligen in Bamberg are possible
sources (interior A. van Stigt, 1986).

324 tram 1 ■

Keizersgracht 508
A.C. Bleys
1881

Picturesque, finely detailed corner property in a free neo-Renaissance eclectic style. The splayed corner with an oriel-tower is the so-called German solution which, in the 19th century, was preferred to the native solution with two gable ends standing at right angles to each other. Recently restored.

325 centre ■

Vondelstraat 140
A.L. van Gendt
1881 Hollandse Manege

Passage, vestibule and beautifully plastered manege with elegant open iron roofing, in what was formerly know as Viennese renaissance and nowadays as International Classicism. Sources: Spanische Reitschule and possibly the Dianabad (K. Etzel, 1842) in Vienna. Large false brackets under the tie-rods and zinc horses' heads. 153 stalls and boxes (altered and partially demolished) integrally supplied by the St. Pancras Iron Work Co. London.

326 tram 1 □

Plantage Middenlaan 53
G.B. Salm & A. Salm
1882 Aquarium Artis Magistra

On the outside: the recently restored
Aquarium with monumental peristyle
and red sandstone base (1882), the
storage buildings in the chalet style
on the Plantage Muidergracht (1875,
1890); the former library and
museum at Plantage Middenlaan 45
(1868); 41-43 – former main building with its rich cast-iron door and
window bars (J. van Maurik, 1855).
Entrance kiosks and railing crowned
with zinc eagles (1854). Director's
house (J.F. Klinkhamer, 1897).

327 tram 9 ☐

Stadhouderskade 41
P.J.H. Cuypers
1877-1885 Rijksmuseum

Built for three purposes: museum of
national history, national art and the
education of artists. Hence the elaborate iconographic programme in the
interior and on the exterior. In spite
of the majestic Gothic silhouette and
fine proportions, the strength of this
'national renaissance' styled building
lies in the detailing rather than in the
handling of space. This is especially
evident in the plan which is based
on Van Campen's Stadhuis (see
147), but misses the latter's compact
handling of space. For the renovation
program by the Spanish architects
Cruz y Ortiz see 636.

328 centre, tram 2, 5 ☐

Singel 446
A. Tepe
1881 Krijtberg

Three-aisled neo-Gothic transeptal basilica of great height. The church is wider at the chancel end than at the narrow street frontage. Tepe worked in a more archaeological Gothic than Cuypers and made little use of modern techniques such as structural ironwork. The church is unique in that its interior decorations have almost completely been preserved. Extremely rich polychromy.

329 centre ☐

Amstel
W. Springer/B. de Greef
1884 Blauwbrug

Like the Hogesluis over the Amstel at the Sarphatistraat inspired by the Alexander III bridge in Paris, but with an adapted iconography. Fine sculptures on the central piers; balustrade in white lime-stone (Comblanchien), cast-iron railings, pedestals in Escauzine stone and columns in highly polished red Swedish granite on which stand bronze lanterns and the imperial crown of Amsterdam.

330 centre ☐

Prinsengracht 739-741
Ed. Cuypers
1884 Melkinrichting

In the 1880's nearly all the important
architects who had been born in the
1850's – Ed. Cuypers, Berlage,
Van Arkel and J.L. Springer – were
working in the Dutch renaissance,
whose decorative, picturesque versat-
ility was quickly seized upon to be
combined with other styles, such as
the timber style used here.

331 centre ■

Haarlemmerweg 10
I. Gosschalk
1885 Imperial Continental Gas
Association/
Westergasfabriek

The Zuiveringshal is one of the
most surprising buildings from the
age of the 'neo'styles. An applied
architecture in freely designed neo-
renaissance which is both rationalist
and picturesque. Ascending arched
corbel courses and narrow high windows make the fronts look slightly
Romanesque. The extensive original
Westergasfabriek was U-shaped and
built around a water tower. A large
part was demolished in the 1960's.
The building is now part of the New
Westerpark (see p. 29).

332 tram 10 □

Kalverstraat 152
H.P. Berlage/Th. Sanders
1886 Focke & Meltzer

Berlage's first large commission,
in association with his partner
Th. Sanders. Venetian renaissance
building with medallions in the spandrels depicting Palissy, Lucca della
Robbia, Wedgewood and the Crabeth
brothers – masters of glass and fai-
ence. The large window-panes behind
freestanding granite columns are
noteworthy. The roof storey on
the Spui side is a later addition.

333 centre ☐

Stationsplein
P.J.H. Cuypers/
A.L. van Gendt/L.J. Eijmer
1882-1889 Centraal Station

Built on a specially constructed
island, which fenced Amsterdam off
from the River IJ. In return Cuypers
gave the city a neo-renaissance
'curtain' on the axis of the Damrak.
The reliefs show allegories of sailing,
trade and industry, and refer to the
classic triumphal arches, making
the central part a triumphal arch for
transport. A complete refurbishing of
the area around the station and the
construction of the north-south metro
line are presently under way.

334 centre ☐

Prins Hendrikkade 76
A.C. Bleys
1885-1887 St. Nicolaas

Aisled transeptal basilica with drome
over crossing, on a tall drum. Striking
baroque interplay of lines between
dome and towers. The articulation of
the towers and the main body of the
church is, however, in a dry neo-
renaissance. Important high altar
(design Bleys, carvings E. van den
Bossche) in well-preserved interior.
Rear looks out on the Oudezijds Kolk
and the paint warehouses Vettewinkel
(W. Hamer, 1899) – one of the most
picturesque 19th century town views.

335 centre ☐

Sarphatipark
J.R. de Kruijff/ L. Beier
Mrs. Stracké-Van Bosse (bust)
1886 Sarphati memorial

The idea of erecting a large statue
to commemorate the 'founder' of the
new Amsterdam' was abandoned in
favour of a fountain with a bust (after
an idea of I. Gosschalk). Baldachino
made of Obernkirchner sandstone,
Swedish granite columns and balusters, bronze bust, capitals, column
base, gargoyles and inscription
tablets.

336 tram 4, 24, 25 ☐

Amstel 115-125
J.P.F. van Rossem/W.J. Vuyk
1887 Circus Oscar Carré

A building which dominates the river
Amstel between the Hogesluis and
the Magere Brug. Circus building
constructed within only a few months,
after an example in Cologne. Roof
span seemingly without visible support and a lively classical front elevation. Narrow, projecting central pavilion and a main façade with striking
ironwork balcony, pilasters, cornice
and attic. Decorations showing grin-
ning clowns, dancers' heads and jest-
ers, by E. van den Bossche and
G. Crevels.

337 centre ☐

Nieuwezijds Voorburgwal 178-180
I. Gosschalk
1885-1888 Die Port van Cleve

Highly refined building. Smooth transition between a renaissance upper
façade and late Gothic: three-point
arches, falchion tracery, Marot strap
work (Louis XIV), oak branches woven
into the shapes of quatrefoils and
falchions (spandrels). On the left the
bodega-façade with important tiled
frieze (Delft Blue) after a design by
A. le Comte.

338 centre ☐

Van Baerlestraat 98
A.L. van Gendt
1886-1888 Concertgebouw

Van Gendt, a salesman among architects, who, if asked, would build in
any style, was proud of not having to
'play the artist'. He was the architect
most in demand in the 1880's and
1890's. He created dignified, if
somewhat arid envelope for Willem
Mengelberg's conductor's baton.
In 1988 the Concertgebouw was
enlarged with a basement under-
neath the whole building and with
a modern gallery and foyer made
of shining materials and glass
(P. de Bruijn).

339 tram 16, 3, 5 ☐

Marnixstraat 148
B. de Greef
1888 Politiebureau Raampoort

The tower behind the building is
situated at the intersection of three
canals – 17th century Bloemgracht
and Singelgracht and the 19th century Hugo de Grootgracht – and offers
interesting urban perspectives. An
example of the solid brick eclecticism
employed by the competent duo De
Greef and his assistant W. Springer.
They built countless schools, fire stations and police stations in this style.

340 tram 10, 13, 14, 17 ☐

Herengracht 380-382
A. Salm
1890 Woonhuis J. Nienhuys

The most luxurious 19th century
residence to be built on the central canals. A 'Petit Chenonceau'
designed in a mixture of early French
renaissance style and the Dutch
equivalent of the New York Francis I
mansion style, such as that of W.K.
Vanderbilt (1880). The façade is
more or less intact but the interior, all
of which was designed by Salm, and
the coach house have been altered.
Now houses the Netherlands Institute
for war documentation.

341 centre □

Koningsplein 1
Th. Schill/D.H. Haverkamp
1891 Verzekeringsgebouw
Kosmos

Tall, elegant building on a narrow
plot. Built as a shop, stores and
offices (1st and 2nd floors) and
dwellings (3rd floor). Renaissance
style with alternating red brickwork
and la Rochette stonework. Rounded
corner with (mutilated) cupola.
In the frieze are ceramic mosaics with
arabesques, gilded inscriptions and
enamelled lava. Lower front mosaic
by H. Elte, c. 1925.

342 centre ■

Keizersgracht 455
J. van Looy
1891 New York/Metz

The 1880's and the 1890's saw the
heyday of the life insurance companies. Architectural prestige was
of considerable importance to them
and they settled conspicuously on
the corners of shopping streets and
squares. The New York Life Insurance
Company prescribed a uniform somewhat pompous baroque-classicism
for its branches. On the roof the
famous Rietveldkoepel (see 441)
under which is a new restaurant
(C. Dam, 1986).

343 centre ☐

Leidseplein 26
J.L. & J.B. Springer/
A.L. van Gendt
1894 Stadsschouwburg

Tailor-made for the decorative talents
of the gifted J.L. Springer. After his
success in London (Frascati in Oxford
Street) in the early 1890s, Springer
returned to Amsterdam to build the
municipal theatre. Due to budget
cuts most of the planned decorations were not executed. After all the
unfavourable criticism passed on the
ultimate result, Springer virtually gave
up his career.

344 centre ☐

Muntplein 2
H.P. Berlage
1895/1911
Nederlanden van 1845

The original, picturesque silhouette was straightened in 1911 by Berlage, resulting in a rectangular block. Built a year after his epoch-making lecture 'Bouwkunst en Impressionisme' (Architecture and Impressionism). Many of the ingredients of the Beurs (see 401) are already present: flat treatment of walls, heavy, expressive stone supports, 'honest' use of materials and sculpture conceived as integral with the architecture.

345 centre ☐

Westerdoksdijk 52
J.F. Klinkhamer/A.L. van Gendt/
A.J. & J. van Stigt/MVRDV
1896 Grain silo/Lofts 2002

From Amsterdam Noord (ferry Distelweg) the silhouette dominates the river IJ. A Modern extension blocks the view of the old building from the Westerdoksdijk. Klinkhamer designed the elevations. Van Gendt checked the thrust of the full silo by means of tension rods, which were heated during construction and then allowed to cool. The ends of the ties are indicated by the cast-iron rosettes. For reconstruction into lofts by Van Stigt and extention by MVRDV, see 638.

346 bus 28 ■

Nieuwe Doelenstraat 2
W. Hamer
1895-1986 Hotel De L'Europe

Hamer has succeeded in giving this
building great stature by the use of
pseudo-pavilions with spout-gables
and pilaster strips – a device borrowed from Centraal Station. Liberal
use of Norwegian granite and Morley
stone. The detailing is a little coarse
and lacks a clear structure but the
building harmonizes well with its
prominent and picturesque site. The
entrance was moved during extension
work in 1911.

347 centre ☐

Keizersgracht 440
W. Hamer
1897
Confectieatelier Van de Waal

Striking building, especially because
of the daringly large windows necessary for the work areas. On the
ground-floor base with recessed
pilaster shafts, there are smooth,
rusticated and Doric columns flanking
the entrance. The windows are set
between 'bi-coloured' lisenes which
are broken by stone decorations and
end in robust orbed pinnacles set
on segmental pediments above the
cornice.

348 centre ☐

Haarlemmerweg 363-367
A. Salm
1897 Ontvangstgebouw
        Vredenhof

Built in Salm's villa style - here crowned with a turret, such as, for example, Villa Corvin (Hilversum) or Ma Retraite (Zeist). Distinguished, staggered building elements, each with its own roof and a plan for the most part symmetrical. Influences from both oriental sources and the English 'country house' style are detectable. The roughcast rendering may be of a later date.

349 tram 10 ☐

Nieuwezijds Voorburgwal 182
C.H. Peters
1895-1899 Hoofdpostkantoor

Derived from the late Gothic Kanselarij in Leeuwarden, this is Peters's largest, if not his most subtle building in the 'post office Gothic' style. Cumbersome when viewed frontally, the building's main volume seems lighter viewed from an acute angle and has a dynamic silhouette. Heavy tower over the loading-bay at the southwest corner. The main hall with galleries and fine colouring is worth a visit. In 1991 the interior was converted in a shopping centre by H. Ruyssenaars.

350 centre ☐

Raadhuisstraat 23-53
A.L. van Gendt
1899 Winkelgalerij Utrecht

The Raadhuisstraat was created in
1894-1896. The arcade accentuates
the broad curve of the street with the
Westertoren (see 130) in the back-
ground. The façade shows influences
of Berlage and Art Nouveau in the
wrought ironwork and stonework,
yet it is traditional in symmetry and
ressaulting of the centre. Crocodiles,
predators etc. summon the passer-
by to purchase life insurances.
The arcade was commissioned by
Insurance Company Utrecht.

351 centre ☐

Jan Luykenstraat 2
Ed. Cuypers
1899 Residence Ed. Cuypers

An important house in the history of
Dutch architecture. Breeding ground
for the Amsterdam School. In the
house itself can be seen the styles
which attracted Cuypers: Norman
Shaw and the English country house
style, a great deal of half-timbering,
an irregular plan and building volume, random placing of windows
and striking Japanese influences,
such as the swept fascia on the
northeast side.

352 centre ■

The twentieth century until 1940

The period 1900-1940 is characterized by a profusion of various architectural movements. One of these movements originated around the turn of the century in the work of an architect who had abandoned the nineteenth century neo-styles and, so, heralded a whole new period in Dutch architecture: Hendrik Petrus Berlage. Berlage advocated an honest and pure architecture. This entailed that structure should be expressed and that ornament should be confined to a supportive role. In spite of this rational approach to architecture, Berlage commanded a rich architectural vocabulary. This ambiguity is expressed in his use of materials, which were both traditional and industrial, and in the sorts of buildings he designed. Berlage had an enormous influence on Dutch architecture and it is, therefore, highly regrettable that much of his work has already been demolished.

Amsterdam School

Around 1912 an architectural movement came into existence: the Amsterdam School. The word 'School' should, in this context, not be taken literally. As the saying goes: 'for every architect there is a style'. The Amsterdam School was born in the office of Ed. Cuypers, in which the architects P.L. Kramer, M. de Klerk and J.M. van der Mey were all working at the beginning of the century. The point of departure was the individual architect's will to form rather than the function of a particular building. The Amsterdam School is characterized by an unbridled fantasy, both in the treatment of surfaces and in the handling of spaces. No form, no matter how eccentric, was eschewed. The decorative potential of building materials, predominantly brickwork, was exploited to the full. Every detail was used to express the style: frames, doors as well as interiors, stained glass, wrought ironwork and so forth. The ideas referred to those of the Gesamtkunstwerk. The buildings themselves are impressive because of the massive, projecting forms and the frequent use of corner towers.

There are several reasons why so much was built in the style of the Amsterdam School. The Dienst Publieke Werken (Local authority Department of Public Works) and the Rijksgebouwendienst (Ministry of Housing and Construction) had Amsterdam School architects in their employment. The Schoonheidscommissie (committee of aesthetics control) had a strong preference for the style. Wendingen, the journal of the authorative architects' association Architectura et Amicitia, was the mouthpiece of the Amsterdam School architects.

De Klerk died in 1923, a tragic loss to the movement. The economic crisis also had its effect: the housing subsidies available under the Housing Act of 1901 were no longer possible and brick became too expensive to be used for extra-vagant designs. The style was modified and lost its expressionist vigour. The Amsterdam School architects were, however, able to maintain their strong position. Architects who put forward other ideas were rewarded with few commissions.

Het Nieuwe Bouwen

The other ideas were, however, in existence and were disseminated internationally. Important sources were the Bauhaus in Germany, Frank Lloyd Wright in the U.S.A. and Le Corbusier in France. In the Netherlands too a generation was growing up with new ideas. It was asserted that architects should not impose their concepts of form at the expense of the function of a building; on the contrary, form should follow function. The architecture of decorative brickwork fell out of favour and structure itself became all important. New building materials such as concrete, steel and glass were frequently used and were admired for their intrinsic value instead of being timidly concealed from view. Concepts such as light, air and direct sunlight became parts of architecture. A building was no longer an inert mass of brick but was, in effect dematerialized. Experiments took place with high-rise buildings and open-block planning. In short, the contrast to the Amsterdam School was total. In 1927, followers of the new trend in Amsterdam, known variously as Nieuwe Zakelijkheid, Het Nieuwe Bouwen or Functionalism, set up De 8, an association which was to act as an interpreter of the new ideas. The manifesto proposed that De 8 was non-aesthetic, non-cubist, non-dramatic and non-romantic.

The architects Merkelbach, Karsten and Groenewegen were among the founding members. In 1928, De 8 merged with the Rotterdam architects' association Opbouw, and in 1934 they joined forces with Groep '32, architects who had ceased to feel at home in Architectura et Amicitia. The admission of Groep '32 gave rise to problems. Conflicts became apparent especially with regard to aesthetics. Some architects remained convinced that good architecture is non-aesthetic; others maintained that each choice of form, no matter how functional, is always a choice for that particular form and for no other, so that an aesthetic element really does enter the scene, albeit by the back door. One of the strongest recalcitrants to defend aesthetics was A. Staal, originally a member of Groep '32. The differences of opinion remained irreconcilable and in 1938 a split took place. In spite of the internal conflicts, however, there was, to a certain extent, a collective attempt to break new ground in architecture. These architects did not have many opportunities to put their ideas into practice. The Delft School which received the majority of new commissions outside Amsterdam, was a conservative, religiously inclined movement which derived inspiration from various traditional sources. One of the most important propagandists for this movement was Granpré Molière, a professor at Delft. It was not until after the Second World War that Functionalism was able to make a breakthrough in Amsterdam. It can be concluded that the years between 1900 and 1940 were among the most turbulent in the architectural history of Amsterdam.

Beursplein
H.P. Berlage
1898-1903 Koopmansbeurs

The Koopmansbeurs (Stock
Exchange) is regarded as one of
the climaxes of Dutch architecture.
Berlage makes a definite break with
the Revivalist styles of the 19th century and replaces it with a rational
building style in which purity of structure is supreme and decoration is
made subservient to the architectural
elements.

401 centre ☐

Beursplein
H.P. Berlage
1898-1903
Koopmansbeurs (interior)

Here it can be clearly seen how
Berlage handled the new technolo-
gies and materials. The steel and
glass roof construction is not concealed but revealed in all its glory.
The side walls refer to medieval structures. The building is now used for
exhibitions and parts of it have been
turned into a concert hall.

402 centre ☐

Henri Polaklaan 9
H.P. Berlage
1899-1900 ANDB

Inspired by an Italian palazzo, the offices of the Diamond Workers' Union reveal Berlage's new concepts of architecture. In the taut treatment of the façade, monotony is avoided by the 'castellations' at roof-level and by the varying window heights. The tower emphasizes the monumentality of the entrance.

403 tram 9, 14 ☐

Leidseplein 28
W. Kromhout
1898-1902 American Hotel

Kromhout is regarded as a forerunner of the Amsterdam School. This is best seen in the American onto which it is not easy to stick a particular style-label. Like Berlage, he rejected the neo-styles, although the style which he developed is rather more expressionist. The popular Café Americain was altered. Annex by G.J. Rutgers.

404 centre ☐

Koningslaan 14-16
K.P.C. de Bazel
1904

An early work by De Bazel in which two aspects are noteworthy: The doorpost-framing and pilasters are expressions of the neo-Renaissance, and the double house is symmetrically planned and divided into a number of equal surfaces. A contrast ensues between De Bazel's abstraction and the naturalism of C. Oosschot, the sculptor.

405 centre ■

Keizersgracht 174-176
G. van Arkel
1905 EHLB

A fine example of Nieuwe Kunst, the Dutch version of Art Nouveau. The building is less taut than his Asscher diamond factory (see 408). In 1969, the Eerste Hollandse Levensverzekerings Bank (Insurance Office) was extended on both sides by C. Wegener Sleeswijk.

406 centre ■

Damrak 28-30
J.F. Staal/J. Kropholler
1904-1906 De Utrecht

One of the few examples of
Americanism in Amsterdam.
Nevertheless, the building adapts
well to the highly varied context
of the Damrak through its modest dimensions. The expressionist
façade sculptures are by J. Mendes
da Costa. The building on the right is
also by Staal and Kropholler (1905),
it's a storehouse for the same insurance company.

407 centre ■

Tolstraat 127-129
G. van Arkel
1907 Asscher

Diamond factory built in a somewhat
austere Art Nouveau, in contrast to
other Amsterdam diamond factories which were built in one of the
Revivalist styles. The building is
impressive for the cantilevered high
wings.

408 tram 4 □

Johannes Vermeerplein
M. de Klerk
1911-1912 Hillehuis

The Hillehuis is regarded as the
first move in the direction of the
Amsterdam School architecture.
The characteristic fantasy is not yet
present. De Klerk was here very much
absorbed in vertical shapes, where
as in his later work horizontal forms
predominate.

409 tram 5 ■

Prins Hendrikkade 108
J.M. van der Mey
1911-1916 Scheepvaarthuis

The Scheepvaarthuis is accepted
as the first true example of the
Amsterdam School style. Van der
Mey was assisted to a great extent by
De Klerk and Kramer. The building is
characterized by strong verticals and
a profusion of expressionist decorations. Since 2007 the building has
been in use as a hotel. The renovation of the interior is credited to Ray
Kentie.

410 centre ☐

Van Beuningenplein
K.P.C. de Bazel
1913-1916

These dwellings are given a particular monumentality by treating the individual unit as an entity. Each dwelling has corner pavilions and a clearly emphasized central entrance. The ornamentation also adds certain grandeur to these dwellings. The decorative elements have an affinity to those of the Nederlandse Handelsmaatschappij (see 416).

411 bus 18 ■

Spaarndammerplantsoen
M. de Klerk
1913-1915 Eigen Haard

De Klerk designed both of the blocks facing the public gardens. The parabolic form of the first of these blocks shows the influence of J.M. Olbrich. The other demonstrates the extent to which the Amsterdam School architects were ruled by what might be called 'brick pleasure' in their purely decorative brickwork as well as in the structural brickwork.

412 bus 22 ■

Dam/Damrak
J.A. van Straaten
1911-1913 De Bijenkorf

One of the first department stores
in the Netherlands to be built in the
neo-classical style. The rear extension, built in the Nieuwe Zakelijkheid
Style by D. Brouwer in 1938, has
been badly mutilated. The multi-
storey car park is by F.J. van Gool,
1980.

413 centre ☐

Zaanstraat/Oostzaanstraat
M. de Klerk
1917-1920 Postkantoor
Spaarndammerplantsoen

This post office, now Amsterdam
School Museum Het Schip, shows the
extent to which De Klerk separated
outward form from function;
the building as autonomous, artistic
expression. The parabola-shaped
window is typical and became popular among the other architects of the
Amsterdam School.

414 bus 22 ☐

Hembrugstraat
M. de Klerk
1917-1920

The tower on the short side of the
housing block has become the
symbol of the Amsterdam School.
Although it serves absolutely no
practical purpose, it has the aesthetic
function of bringing the two wings
together to create a coherent whole.

415 bus 22 ■

Vijzelstraat 30-34
K.P.C. de Bazel
1919-1926 Nederlandse
Handelsmaatschappij

De Bazel's masterpiece. The use of
different sorts of brick and stone and
the staggering of the façade achieve
a strong sense of movement. The
commonest criticism of the building
maintains that it is too large in relation to the adjoining canal houses
which are pushed aside by the enormous mass of brick and stone.
Now home of the Amsterdam
Archives. The interior was renovated
by Claus and Kaan Architects.

416 centre ☐

Baarsjesweg/Postjesweg
A.J. Westerman
1922 4e Ambachtsschool

During the 1920s and '30s the
Public Works Department designed
countless school buildings.
N. Lansdorp, P.L. Marnette and
A.J. Westerman were among the most
influential architects employed by
the department. The school on
Baarsjesweg shows the symmetrical,
hierarchic plan typical of Westermans
designs. The sculptures at the
entrance are by Hildo Krop, civic
sculptor.

417 tram 7, 17 ■

Reguliersbreestraat 26
H.L. de Jong
1918-1921 Tuschinski

This cinema occupies a special place
in the architecture of Amsterdam.
Some consider it to be a fine example of Art Deco while others see it as
pure Kitsch. The exuberant forms of
the exterior continue into the luxurious foyer which gives the visitor
the feeling that, for a while, he has
escaped from everyday reality.
The building is recently restored.

418 centre ☐

Vrijheidslaan 10 etc.
M. de Klerk
1921-1922

Only the façade of this block was designed by De Klerk. The use of convex and concave shapes has led, however, to a strong sculptural quality. The balconies on their different levels have been ingeniously linked together. In 1936 the windows had to be enlarged because of the poor lighting.

419 tram 25 ■

Roelof Hartplein
J. Boterenbrood
1922-1927 Huize Lydia

Boterenbrood was a second generation Amsterdam School architect. The expressionism of the first generation disappeared. In Huize Lydia, Boterenbrood has tried, without completely succeeding, to fuse the separate volumes into one.

420 tram 5 ■

Henriëtte Ronnerplein
M. de Klerk
1921-1923

De Klerk showed little concern for the function of these idiosyncratically shaped houses. His remarkable genius directed its powers of fantasy to outward appearances rather than to the user. Note the small windows.

421 tram 4 ■

P.L. Takstraat
P.L. Kramer
1921-1922 Dageraad

Kramer designed this housing complex in collaboration with De Klerk, Kramer being responsible for the dwellings and De Klerk for the corner element. Kramer, one of the most original Amsterdam School architects, achieved here a peak of sculptural architecture. No effort was spared in the creation of this imposing complex.

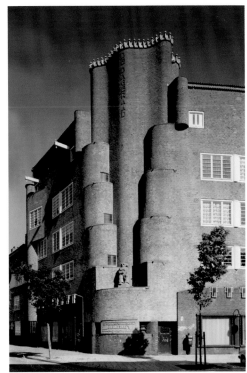

422 tram 4 ■

Betondorp-Brink
D. Greiner
1921-1926

Greiner designed most of the northern section of this garden-suburb. Unique is its village-like character. The low-rise housing has gardens – at that time an unprecedented luxury for the working class. Despite the limited budget, the result is more than satisfactory. This suburb was recently renovated.

423 tram 9 ■

Betondorp-Onderlangs
J. Gratama/J.H. Mulder
1922

In Betondorp cheaper methods of building were investigated, leading to the use of new materials and techniques. Roughly a thousand dwellings were built using prefabricated concrete components. Apart from Greiner and Gratama, W. Greve – Oogststraat (1923) and Van Loghem, the advocate of Nieuwe Zakelijkheid, – Schovenstraat (1926).

424 tram 9 ■

J.M. Coenenstraat
J.F. Staal
1922-1923

After a 'Berlagian' period Staal was converted to the Amsterdam School. He was inspired by De Klerk and Kramer, as can be seen on the corner of the Barth. Ruloffstraat and at the rear of this block. The J.M. Coenenstraat side shows a tauter, more personal style. The flats opposite on the corner of the Beethovenstraat and the Apollolaan are also by Staal (1939).

425 tram 5, 24 ■

Hacquartstraat
F.A. Warners
1924

Like Staal, Warners was also converted to the Amsterdam School after a Berlagian period. The form is unmistakable even though the brickwork, characteristic of the Amsterdam School is here, concealed behind a layer of grey plaster. There is fine detailing, especially in the doors and the chequerboard decoration.

426 tram 16 ■

Smaragdstraat
J.C. van Epen
1922-1924

Like so many others, Van Epen occupies a distinct position within the Amsterdam School. This block on the Smaragdstraat is distinguished by a rather robust vertical emphasis. Even more striking, however, is the use of colours, green and mustard-yellow, which makes the work of Van Epen immediately recognizable.

427 tram 4 ■

Droogbak 1
P.L. Marnette
1925 Schipperskinderenschool

Marnette was one of the architects employed by the Public Works Department (DPW). The DPW built a large number of schools in the style of the Amsterdam School. This school is modestly decorated but satisfying because of the slender proportions and sculptural forms.

428 centre ■

Boerhaaveplein/A. Bonnstraat 30
A.J. Westerman
1920-1921 Badhuis

One of the many characteristic bath
houses built by the Public Works
Department (DPW). There is an
identical one on the Smaragdplein.
Even such small, purely functional
buildings were built in the style of the
Amsterdam School. Nowadays such
bath houses are becoming obsolete.

429 metro Weesperplein ■

Mercatorplein
H.P. Berlage
1925-1927

Late work of Berlage. Originally,
Berlage was opposed to the
Amsterdam School but because of
the disappearance of expressionism
in the work of the Amsterdam School
and because Berlage suppressed the
rational element in this scheme to
a certain extent, the distinction
between the two became less
clearly defined. Berlage's ideas about
the design of squares are clearly
expressed here. Renovated in the
1990s.

430 tram 13 □

Tuindorp Nieuwendam
Purmerweg
B.T. Boeyinga
1925-1927

As in many of the garden towns, a central square forms the heart of the town plan in which raised gatehouses are built. In this period Boeyinga was working for the Municipal Housing Department. This garden town is now regarded as the apex in the rustic variant of the Amsterdam School. Its low structures and plentiful greenery are characteristic.

431 bus 32 ■

Tolstraat 154
J.A. Brinkman/L.C. van der Vlugt
1926-1931

The administration building for the Theosophical Society was built by Brinkman and Van der Vlugt in 1926. The assembly hall with its unusual shape was built five years later. Both buildings are now a library. Despite their common roots these buildings show differences from post-war functionalism.

432 tram 4 ☐

Amstel/Vrijheidslaan
H.P. Berlage
1926-1932 Berlagebrug

The bridge is part of a complex which also embraces the embankment buildings along the Weesperzijde and the Amsteldijk. The tower, with sculptures by Hildo Krop, is the dominant element. The bridge itself, as might be expected of Berlage, is on the austere side. Decoration can be seen in the use of materials and colours (the Amsterdam colours of red and black).

433 tram 4, 12 □

Jacob Obrechtplein
H. Elte
1928 Synagogue

This synagogue shows evidence of W.M. Dudok's influence, but, nevertheless, has a strong individual character. The influence of Frank Lloyd Wright can also be detected; especially in the flat canopy above the entrance. The decorative wrought-iron entrance gate is a little incongruous.

434 tram 16 ■

Olympiaplein
P.L. Kramer
1928 Bridge

From 1917 onwards Kramer, now
employed by the Public Works
Department, designed a large
number of the bridges made necessary throughout the entire city by the
enormous increase in traffic.
The bridges were designed in the
Amsterdam School style. The actual
structure is enclosed in a covering
of brick and stone sculptures are by
Hildo Krop. Amsterdams Lyceum:
H.A.J. & J. Baanders (1920).

435 tram 24 metro ring ☐

Nieuwezijds Voorburgwal 225
J.F. Staal
1927-1929 De Telegraaf

Staal did not simply continue in
the style of the Amsterdam School
(see 425). This former office building for newspaper De Telegraaf is
evidence of a new phase in his work.
Rationalism becomes dominant; the
transition to Functionalism is obvious.
The façade is symmetrical and
balanced. In 2004 a replica of the
sculptural group of newspaper boys
by Hido Krop was restored to its
place.

436 centre ■

Cliostraat 36-40
J. Duiker
1929-1930 Openluchtschool

Duiker's intention in this school
was to make full use of the sun. He
achieved this through the use of
glass, steel and concrete, and by
situating a low janitor's lodge on the
southern side of the site. The result
is an open structure in which the user
of the building occupies a central
position.

437 tram 5, 2 ∎

Victorieplein
J.F. Staal
1929-1930 De Wolkenkrabber

With this masterpiece Staal took the
decisive step to Nieuwe Bouwen.
It was the first high-rise housing
block in Amsterdam, but did not
consist of a dull stacking of identical
floors. The glazed staircase above
the entrance, flanked by balconies
is an eye-catcher. This architectural
treatment gives the building a rising
feeling.

438 tram 4 ∎

Stadionplein
J. Wils
1926-1928 Olympisch Stadion

Wils was strongly influenced by
Frank Lloyd Wright among others.
Unfortunately, the Citroën building
(1929-1931) has been drastically
rebuilt. The Olympic Stadium, which
he built with C. van Eesteren has
remained relatively intact. It is
completely restored now. Wils also
designed the post-war Citroën building (1959) at the other side.

439 tram 16 ☐

Gerrit van der Veenstraat 99
N. Lansdorp
1930

Early example of the rising Delft
School. The Delft School shows the
influence of Berlage, especially in the
choice of materials, but also derives
inspiration from Swedish architecture. Later, traditional sources are
mobilized.

440 centre ■

Keizersgracht 455
G.Th. Rietveld
1933 Rietveldkoepel

The lightweight steel and glass structure contrasts vividly with the 19th century building (see 343) on which it stands. It offers superb views of the city in almost all directions. The shop front to Keizersgracht 449 is also by Rietveld (1938).

441 centre ☐

Reguliersbreestraat 31
J. Duiker
1934 Cineac

Duiker believed that the living medium of the film (especially news films) should spill out onto the street. The auditorium was entered directly from the street. From the outside it was possible to see the projectors on the first floor. In 1980 Cineac was literally decapitated but a reconstruction also of the steel scaffolding with its neon advertising – an essential part of the total design – followed.

442 centre ☐

Apollolaan/Stadionweg
A. Boeken
1933-1935 Apollohal

The Apollohal, originally built for sport
and exhibitions is a good example
of Nieuwe Zakelijkheid. The façades,
for the most part glazed, give the hall
a degree of transparancy. Renovation
has, however, ruined this aspect and
effectively robs bed the hall of its
strength. The adjoining Apollo pavilion is in the same style.

443 tram 24 ☐

Uiterwaardenstraat
Zanstra, Giesen en Sijmons
1934

Two blocks of steel-framed dwellings.
One block has studio apartments
and the other dwellings only.
The independence of both blocks
is emphasized by the different balconies.

444 tram 25 ■

Valeriusstraat 55
L.H.P. Waterman
1935

On the ground floor is business accommodation and above living areas. Both have their own well-designed entrances. The house itself is older than 1935, the year in which the existing façade was replaced in the style of the Nieuwe Zakelijkheid – a style which in no way detracts from the adjoining properties.

445 tram 2 ■

Weesperplein 1
J.F. Staal
1935 Joodse Invalide

This building is characterized by a great transparancy. The corner element with its original crown is the dominant element and is apparently supported on thin columns.
The entrance is emphasized by the canopy and a series of round windows.

446 metro Weesperplein □

Albrecht Dürerstraat
W. van Tijen
1936 Montessori School

That this school was inspired by
Duiker's Openluchtschool (see 437)
is immediately evident. Both buildings exploited steel and glass to
achieve good lighting. The main
difference is that Duiker's building
is situated inside a closed housing-
block whereas this Montessori School
stands in full sunlight.

447 tram 5, 24 ■

Lekstraat 61-63
A. Elzas
1936 Synagogue

The angularity of the stone-faced
façade with its low-placed windows
gives this building a sacred character
in keeping with its original function.
The annexe has elements directly
borrowed from Le Corbusier.

448 tram 25 ■

Anthony van Dijkstraat 4-12
W. van Tijen/M. Stam &
L. Stam-Beese/H. Maaskant
1936 Drive-in houses

The drive-in houses, linked to the
gymnasium of the Montessori School
(see 447) belong to the few row
houses to be built in the Nieuwe
Zakelijkheid style before the Second
World War. Their thin walls and light
structure give the impression of openness while their discreet proportions
enable them to merge into the street
scene.

449 tram 5, 24 ■

Bestevaerstraat/
J. van Stolbergstraat
B. Merkelbach/Ch.J.F. Karsten
1937

Bos en Lommer saw the first use of
open-block housing in Amsterdam.
Previous development had always
been in closed blocks. The advantage
of the open block is that each dwelling can receive sunlight. After the
Second World War the closed block
was almost entirely superseded by
the open block.

450 tram 12, 14 ■

Apollolaan 15
D. Roosenburg
1937-1939
Sociale Verzekeringsbank

From whichever side this building is approached, its dominant character cannot be denied. The tall, slender block linked to the flattened slab provides a strong image. However, the building is not entirely functional. The exterior is faced with stone and the interior is provided with expensive decorative finishes.

451 tram 5, 24 ■

Hoofddorpweg/Sloterkade
Zanstra, Giesen en Sijmons
1939

In this block of flats too great a severity is avoided by bending the corner outwards. This device is also used on the roof, thus giving the corner element as a whole a less heavy impression. Decoration is restricted to the balcony railings.

452 tram 2 ■

Bernhardplein
H.G.J. Schelling
1939 Amstel Station

Schelling designed a large number
of stations for the Dutch Railways
of which Amstel Station and
Muiderpoort Station are among the
best examples. The high level of
daylight penetration and the spacious
effect of the hall are typical.
The murals, which are related to
the railways, are by Peter Alma.

453 metro 51, 53, 54 □

A. Fokkerweg 2
J.W. van Tijen/H. Maaskant
1939 Nationaal Luchtvaart
Laboratorium

This building, which is now called the
Aviation and Space Laboratory, could
be called a compromise between different styles. On one side traditional
brickwork is used while the other side
is in thoughtfully applied reinforced
concrete. Pure functionalism is, thus,
somewhat softened without lapsing
into traditionalism.

454 tram 2 ■

The twentieth century 1940 to 1990

In the period before the Second World War much theoretical and experimental work had been done, which, because of the outbreak of the war, could not be executed immediately. During the war period, architects from various styles formed a group, the Kerngroep voor Woningarchitectuur, which concerned itself with the question of how social building should be tackled after the war and how to make up the lost ground of the war. Though the Delft School was strongly represented in this group, preference was given to designing and building according to ideas, determined for the greater part by the functional theories of the Nieuwe Zakelijkheid.

In 1945, when the Second World War was over, the damage turned out to be enormous. However, during the first years after the war hardly any attention was paid to housing. There was little material and the stimulation of the economic recovery was given preference to: ports were rebuilt and industry was put on its feet again. At the beginning of the 1950's a start was made with housing in Amsterdam. In spite of the shortage of money and building materials building had to be carried out on a large scale and at a high pace in order to cope with the huge housing shortage. Apart from post-war reconstruction an exploding population and a growing economy had to be dealt with.

Algemeen Uitbreidingsplan

The pre-war General Development Plan for Amsterdam (AUP) for the gradual, balanced expansion of Amsterdam until the year 2000 had decided that the centre of Amsterdam would have a city centre function and that new residential areas would be built on the outskirts of the town. In the city centre, mainly offices would be built, easily accessible as a result of the building of wide roads, for which buildings were to be demolished. The plans for the garden cities to the south and west had already been laid down in the AUP. The principles of CIAM (a group of international architects united in the Congrès Internationaux d'Architecture Moderne) had great influence on these plans. Acceptance of new construction methods and ideas about the building of new residential areas with much light and communal greenery, led to the so-called open-block housing in the plans for Slotermeer. After the war, however, the open blocks were replaced by a plan with L-shaped blocks. This method of building was put into practice for the first time in 1947 when the Frankendaal area was developed.

In 1950 a start was made with housing in Slotermeer. Many architects were involved in the building of this suburb. However, they were hardly able to realize their architectural ideals because of the influence of the State with its subsidy arrangements. The strong interference and frugality of the State meant that not much was left of the original architectural designs.

The next suburb to be built was Geuzenveld. It was decided to divide the area into 6 large sections and to nominate a well-known architect for each section who was commissioned to design 600-1000 dwellings. The architects, who received these large commissions, were W.M. Dudok, B. Bijvoet, B. Merkelbach, J.H. van den Broek (with J. Bakema), W. van Tijen and C. Wegener-Sleeswijk. The architectural firm of Th.J. Lammers was commissioned to construct housing for special groups. They remained dependent on state subsidies and approval, however, and the architecture produced was undistinguished. The ideas of Nieuwe Bouwen (Functionalism) lost much of their strength when they were translated into actual buildings. The rationality of Functionalism was emphasized more and more. New materials such as concrete, steel and glass made it possible to prefabricate building elements, so that system building could be put to use. This was faster and reduced labour costs. The strong preference for high-rise building originated from the idea, that in this way space and material were used rationally, and that social services were accessible in the most economical manner. Prefabricated construction was encouraged by the government in the development of the third garden city: Slotervaart. Since 1954 around 10.000 dwellings have been built. The number of high-rise flats has increased; in the fourth and most westerly garden city, Osdorp, high-rise dwellings accounted for more than a quarter of the total.

FORUM

Towards the end of the fifties opposition grew to the emphasis that functionalism placed on pragmatism. The editorship of the architectural magazine FORUM was taken over by architects such as A. van Eyck, J.B. Bakema, H. Hertzberger and D.C. Apon. These FORUM architects pointed out the importance of the relationship between people and architecture. One should build with the idea that a town is a cluster, a combination of all kinds of parts connected to each other with the casbah as the example to be followed. This view of architecture found expression in the Burgerweeshuis (Municipal Orphanage) by A. van Eyck (1960). A great deal of building, however, still had to be done urgently. In 1967 a plan based on CIAM ideas to build on a large scale in the Bijlmermeer was put into practice. Building flats of eleven storeys on a hexagonal grid led to a honeycomb arrangement. A great deal of criticism was levelled at this wholesale approach to housing and it was asserted that other forms of building should be considered. It also became clear that the population of Amsterdam was decreasing. Amsterdammers were not moving into the newly-built areas on the outskirts, but to the satellite towns. Pressure from protesting citizens forced the city council to revise its vision of the city.

Urban Renewal

At the beginning of the 1970's the decision was made to improve the quality of life in the city. In order to reinforce the residential function of the city centre, a plan was made in which building in and for existing neighbourhoods was central. The policy of demolition was replaced by a 'renovation policy'. Half way through the 1970's the first urban renewal projects were executed and in the eighties this has remained an important part of the building policy. Many architects, who produced designs for these projects, were influenced by the ideas of the FORUM architects. They build on a small scale, imaginatively and with many details. Architects searching for pragmatism and rationality, such as C. Weeber and P. de Bruijn, reacted against this small-scale, detailed approach.

In addition to the large-scale office building and the small-scale housing construction of the 1980's, a number of large-scale housing construction projects were also undertaken. A start was made on the north bank of the IJ: Rem Koolhaas drew up an urban development plan for the IJ-plein. Large housing complexes have been designed on the eastern islands on both sides of the Wittenburgervaart.

But the most significant housing developments took place to the west and south-west of the city. Here tens of thousands of dwellings were built in the Middenveldsche Akerpolder and in the market-gardening area of Sloten. Architects and urban developers have learnt from the errors made in the Bijlmermeer. In designing these larger areas, ensuring public safety has played an important role. Variations in building form and the use of colour are intended to help improve the quality of life. In the 1990's building in Amsterdam can take on many forms. On the one hand, functional, ultra-modern office and business property is being built and, on the other hand, the smallest sites in street façades are being filled up, as part of the urban renewal programme. The selection that follows tries to illustrate this.

Korte Geuzenstraat 98
J.W.H.C. Pot & J.F. Pot-Keegstra
1942 Oranjehof

In 1939 the decision was made to build the Oranjehof, one of the first complexes for single people. In 1942 the building was finished: 108 dwellings for unmarried working women. The façade, the most interesting side of which is along the Geuzenkade, shows a rather traditional way of building in brick, with brick arches above the windows.

501 tram 12, 13, 14 ■

Da Costakade (next to) 158
B. Merkelbach/P. Elling
1950 Tetterode

The extension of the Type-Foundry 'Amsterdam' – N. Tetterode, is an early example of the association between the architects Merkelbach and Elling. Merkelbach started working on the extension with Ch.J.F. Karsten however. The building is constructed in concrete, steel and glass and is now occupied by squatters who have set up workshops and studios.

502 tram 17 ■

E. de Roodestraat 14-16
G.H.M. Holt
1952 St. Josefkerk

Bos and Lommer was the first area
of the AUP to be realized. Together
with K.P. Tholens, Holt built a Roman
Catholic Church, in which the change
in church-building since the Second
World War was expressed. The concrete skeleton, which in the interior
has an infill of Limburg stone and
dressed concrete panels, is clearly
visible. The stained-glass windows
are by M. de Leeuw. It now houses
a climbing centre called 'Between
heaven and earth'.

503 bus 47 □

J. Bottemastraat
A. van Eyck
1953

The social aspect of these old people's homes was central for Van Eyck.
He worked on this project in association with architect J. Rietveld. They
linked together a number of houses
of a similar type to create a plan
which uses the house as well as the
space around it as part of the design.

504 tram 13 ■

Bos en Lommerplein 25
M.F. Duintjer
1956 Opstandingskerk/Kolenkit

This church in Amsterdam West got its nickname 'the Coal-scuttle' from its characteristic tower. Duintjer's aim was to create cohesion between the various parts of the complex: vicarage, tower, community centre areas and church hall. The latter is lit by high, diagonally placed windows. Light plays an important part in the interior of the church.

505 tram 13 □

Comeniusstraat
J.F. Berghoef
1959 flats

As part of the Slotervaart development, Berghoef designed a number of blocks of flats, which can be seen from the Cornelis Lelylaan. He used the Airey industrial building system which consists of a steel skeleton, concrete wall panels and timber floors. This offers the architect a great many opportunities for variation. Berghoef built these flats partly over water.

506 tram 1 ■

Stadhouderskade 85
B. Merkelbach/M. Stam
1959 Geïllustreerde Pers

This building has a glazed curtain wall, on which the windowcleaners' rails provide a certain amount of diversion. The setbacks in the façade emphasize the structure. The building is presently used by the municipal Registry Office.

507 tram 16, 24, 25 □

Bos en Lommerplantsoen 1
B. Merkelbach/P. Elling
1960 GAK (UWV)

The bringing together of the General Administration Offices under one roof involved close cooperation between Merkelbach and Elling (design), Bodon (construction) and Van Eesteren (town planning). This long building constructed in steel, glass, curtain walls and prefabricated concrete floors is divided into two by the projecting central block. Parts of the building are temporarily being used as artist's studios. Its future use is presently under consideration.

508 tram 7, 14 ■

IJsbaanpad 3
A. van Eyck
1960 Burgerweeshuis

With this former municipal orphanage, Van Eyck, a leading figure in the FORUM-movement built a monument expressing his abhorrence of func-tional inhumanity, to which, in his opinion, the Nieuwe Zakelijkheid had descended. The orphanage is being restored by Aldo van Eyck and transformed into offices. The Tripolis building nextdoor is a later creation 1992 of the Van Eycks.

509 tram 16, metro 50 ■

Overtoom 557
C. de Geus/J.B. Ingwersen
1961

This business premise with their curved façades on concrete piloti is clearly inspired by the Unité d'Habitation of Le Corbusier. Originally, Autopon, the garage-concern, was established on the ground floor. Above, there are five layers of split-level apartments.

510 tram 1 □

Apollolaan 141
H. Salomonson
1961 villa

This villa on columns shows some affinity with the Villa Savoye in Poissy (Le Corbusier, 1929) and betrays Le Corbusier's influence on the architect. With a terrace and copious use of glass, the architect intended to create a relationship between the interior and the outside world.

511 bus 66-69 ■

De Cuserstraat 3
M.F. Duintjer
1963 School

Duintjer was an architect who combined the ideas of the Nieuwe Zakelijkheid and the Delft School. This building, situated beside a canal on the corner of the Buitenveldertse-laan, has a concrete skeleton with floors projecting through the façade. On the top of the building is a revolving observatory.

512 tram 5, metro 51 ■

Prinses Irenestraat 36
K.L. Sijmons
1966 Thomaskerk

Most of the concrete structure of
this church, which is inspired by
Le Corbusier's chapel at Ronchamp,
is faced with bricks and tiles. In
the interior, however, the concrete
structure is exposed. The unique
artwork of glass in sanctuary is by the
Spanish painter A. Saura.

513 tram 5 □

Weesperstraat 7-57
H. Hertzberger
1966 Student flats/restaurant

Along the Weesperstraat, which was
widened after the war, Hertzberger
built flats and facilities for students.
A broad interior street has been provided on the fourth floor. The outside
world is, as it were, supposed to
penetrate into the building and this
does actually occur on the ground
floor.

514 metro 51, 53, 54 □

Van Nijenrodeweg
W.M. Dudok
1967 flats

Dudok, in association with the office
of Kromhout and Groet, designed a
street wall, in which high and low-rise
buildings alternate. A fine succession
has been created of yellow and black
façades and the higher white blocks
of flats by K. Molman.

515 metro 51, tram 5 ■

Buikslotermeerplein/Het Breed
(surr.)
Oyevaar/Stolle/Van Gool
1967 Plan Van Gool/Noord

For a competition in 1962 Van Gool
designed five blocks of flats. He was
awarded the commission to carry
out the plan that was named after
him. The flats are reached through
two 'gallery streets' within the building volume. The blocks are linked by
overhead bridges.

516 bus 30, 36, 37 □

Frederiksplein
M.F. Duintjer
1968 Nederlandsche Bank

On the site of the former 'Paleis voor Volksvlijt' is now a large bank building, noticeable because of its 17 floors. This office tower is surrounded by a rectangular building of 3 and 4 storeys. The complex has been expanded with a second tower, designed by J. Abma on the axis of the Utrechtsestraat.

517 centre ■

Basisweg 52
J.P. Kloos
1969 Reesink & Co.

Warehouse with office and showroom for the firm of Reesink & Co. in Sloterdijk. As space had to be kept free for a railway, one of the corners of the building rests on columns. The large glazed area in the façade of the warehouse was intended to provide the workers with natural light.

518 bus 232, metro 50 ■

Dijkgraafplein
J.P. Kloos
1970

The western end of Tussenmeer is
formed by a housing and shopping
complex by Kloos. The dwellings are
reached by means of glazed galleries
which serve four floors. These galleries also connect the blocks.

519 tram 1 ■

Singel 428
A. Cahen/J.P.H.C. Girod
1970

Built as an infill on a site in the
existing canal façade, this property
was designed in precast concrete
elements. Great attention was paid,
however, to fitting the building into
its historic context with regard to
scale and articulation.

520 centre ■

Badhuisweg
A. Staal
1971 Overhoeks Shell

The new Shell research laboratory was built on the north side of the IJ with extensive use of plastic building materials. The most striking characteristic is, however, the tower, built on piloti and situated diagonally to the bank of the river IJ. Now part of a large-scale reconstruction plan for the north bank of the IJ, the building will shortly become the site for various smaller offices.

521 ferry ■

De Boelelaan 1105
Architectengroep '69
1973 Vrije Universiteit

The main building, which accommodates a great number of general facilities, the humanities and social sciences, is largely built of concrete. The façade of the sixteen-storeyed tower are given relief by the balcony constructions that run round the entire building. Several floors are taken up by a restaurant. The carillon on the roof is a striking detail.

522 tram 5, metro 51 ■

Bickersgracht 210-218
P. de Ley/J. van den Bout
1975

After the war Bickerseiland was
scheduled for the building of business premises. In 1970 protest
actions were started by the residents.
The result was that part of the island
was reserved for housing. De Ley
and Van den Bout designed eighteen
deep houses, with lighting achieved
by means of light wells.

523 centre ■

Oude Schans 3
H. Zeinstra
1977

Zeinstra has completed many infill
projects in existing street and canal
façades. With regard to scale and
proportion, this house fits in well
between the canal houses. The
façade is, in facto made up of two
screens, the front one of which is
white and leans forward. The window
openings in this screen do not com-
ply with those in the second, light
grey façade. Oriel-like windows unite
the two screens.

524 centre ■

Weteringschans 26-28
F.J. van Gool
1979 Kantoorvilla's

On the site of two former 19th century villas, Van Gool designed these office villas, of which the ground floor area was not to be bigger than that of its predecessors. These concrete buildings, cantilevered out at several points, were faced with brick and the windows, flush with the façade, were all of the same size. There has been much criticism of these offices. Seen from the Stadhouderskade, the buildings look very different.

525 centre ■

Prinsengracht 151
S. Soeters
1980

In 1850 two warehouses were converted into a school: Louise-Bewaarschool (I. Warnsinck). They were provided with a new, eclectic façade, typical of the middle of the 19th century. When the entire building was rebuilt in 1978-1980, this façade was retained and now works as a free-standing screen. Seven houses and a courtyard were built behind the façade. The hall disappeared to make way for a light well. The façade was painted salmon-pink.

526 centre ■

Plantage Middenlaan 33
A. van Eyck
1981 Hubertushuis

St. Hubertus Society's reception and
advisory centre for single parents
and their children accommodated in
the so-called Moederhuis, consisting
partly of a 19th century building and
partly of a new building. The old and
the new parts are connected by a
transparent staircase and united both
inside and outside by a rich use of
colour. The architect intended that
this house, in which the small scale
and richness of detail are noteworthy,
should above all be well adapted to
the users and emphasize humane-
ness.

527 tram 9, 14 ■

Academisch Medisch Centrum
M.F. Duintjer/D.J. Istha/
J.H. Kramer/T. van Willigen/
D. van Mourik
1981

The AMC, built to replace a number
of hospitals in the city centre, also
houses the medical faculties of
Amsterdam University. The interior
of the large complex is especially
interesting; an entire city with interior
streets and squares, covered by roof-
lights. As well as terraces, restaurants
and shops the AMC provides accommodation for a large collection of
modern art.

528 metro 50, 54 ■

Europaplein
A. Bodon
1981 RAI

The first part of this exhibition complex was built in 1961. Several extensions have been built, the last of which in 1981, resulted in a series of light and functional looking halls. The external walls are made up of solid and glazed horizontal bands above which is a sloping plane of translucent panelling. Sometimes it has its own white colour and sometimes it reflects the blue of the sky.

529 tram 4 ■

Nieuwe Houttuinen
H. Hertzberger/A. van Herk/
K. Nagelkerke
1982

This site, which was originally scheduled for a four-lane highway has been designed by several different architects. The dwellings with their fronts facing into the internal street and their backs facing the Houttuinen are by Hertzberger. The blocks by Van Herk and Nagelkerke are on the opposite side of this street. They have plastered insulation over a concrete frame and brickwork infill. The point-block was designed by EGM.

530 centre ■

IJ-plein
J. Voorberg, Van Meer, Archi-
tectengroep '69 and others,
general plan R. Koolhaas
1982

Office for Metropolitan Architecture
was commissioned to design the
lay-out of the former ADM shipyard
site, situated on the north bank of
the river IJ. In association with J.
Voorberg, Koolhaas created a pattern
of villa-like blocks, in combination
with strip-blocks. The further development of this plan was left to the individual architects. Especially noteworthy are the stuccoed, urban villas by
Van Meer. The two stripblocks were
designed by Architectengroep '69.

531 ferry IJplein ■

Zuiderkerkhof/
St. Antoniesbreestraat
H. Hagenbeek/Th. Bosch
1983-1984 Pentagon

For this site, under which the metro
runs, Bosch designed a housing
complex in the form of a pentagon.
Next to the 'Pentagon' is an archway
leading to the Zuiderkerkhof (churchyard of the Zuiderkerk). This pleasant
square and the surrounding housing
were designed by Hagenbeek.

532 centre (square) ■

W. Witsenstraat 12-14
H. Hertzberger
1983 Apollo scholen

Grouped round a communal square
are three schools whose villa-like
appearance enables them to har-
monize with their surroundings.
The Montessori School and the
Willemspark School, both in concrete
blockwork, are by Hertzberger. The
third school is by Van de Pol. The
two Hertzberger schools have an
identical basic shape which consists
of a square with classrooms in the
four corners grouped round a central
hall. Variations in detailing and in the
positions of the windows give each
school its own identity.

533 tram 16 ■

Zwanenburgwal
P. de Ley/F. Roos
1984

De Ley, while improving a dilapi-
dated section of the Zwanenburgwal
opposite the Stopera (see 548), has
tried to preserve the character of the
old canal front. The scheme involved
restoration and conversion as well as
new building. The stuccoed façades
are important elements in the design.
Especially, the block on the corner of
the Staalstraat which is built around
a courtyard, offers a stimulating play
of rendered surfaces.

534 centre ■

J. Catskade 64
K. de Kat/D. Peek/H. Zeinstra
1984

The five-storeyed block on the
J. Catskade, designed by H. Zeinstra,
is set at an acute angle with the
façade on the Wittenstraat which
decreases from four to two storeys.
At the corner the two blocks merge
into each other and are linked by a
striking little building through which
the ends of the access galleries
project.

535 tram 10 ■

Spuistraat/Singel
Th. Bosch
1984 P.C. Hoofthuis

Bosch designed a building known as
the P.C. Hoofthuis which follows the
building-lines of both the Spuistraat
and the Singel. The Witte Huis (see
354) has been skilfully absorbed into
the design by means of similarities in
size and colour. Giving priority to
the functionality of the building has
resulted in the clarity of the design.

536 centre ■

Venserpolder
C. Weeber
1984 Plan

This plan, which Weeber designed for 3800 dwellings in the Venserpolder was further worked out by different architects in accordance with definite guidelines. The block, which is divided into horizontal layers and decorated with a number 1, is by Weeber himself.

537 metro 53 ■

Sloterdijk Station
H. Reijnders
1986 station

A number of new stations were necessitated by the new orbital railway-line around Amsterdam. The design for Sloterdijk by Reijnders makes dramatic use of glass, steel and plastics. The station building and concourse are covered by a steel structure which floats like a tabletop above the buildings. The railway lines are on different levels. Reijnders has used several post-modern elements.

538 metro 50, tram 12, 14 ■

Ambonplein
H. Hertzberger
1986 De Evenaar

This freestanding primary school
catches the eye in the midst of the
local brickwork housing for its colour
and use of materials. It consists of
three layers and has curved façades
with much glass. In the heart of the
building is a meeting area.

539 tram 3 ■

Waterlooplein
W. Holzbauer/C. Dam/B. Bijvoet
1986-1987 Stadhuis-
Muziektheater (Stopera)

In 1968 Holzbauer won the competition for a new city hall in Amsterdam.
An opera building was being planned
for another site in the city. Both projects were undergoing difficulties and
in 1979 the idea arose of combining
the two buildings. The 'Stopera' built
by C. Dam at one of the most attractive sites along the river Amstel.

540 centre ■

Foppingadreef/Hoogoorddreef
A. Alberts/M. van Huut
1987 NMB (now ING-bank)

The former head office of the
Nederlandse Middenstandsbank was
designed from the anthroposophical
point of departure that states that
nature provides the example to be
followed by architecture. The result
is an S-shaped complex of linked,
brick-clad, concrete towers. The pentagon is an important element in this
energy-saving building. Right angles
hardly occur.

541 metro 50, 54 ■ (on request)

Realengracht/Vierwindenstraat
L. Lafour and R. Wijk
1989

With this project won Lafour and Wijk
the Merkelbach Prize in 1991. Based
on a nineteenth-century example,
this complex of 66 dwellings is built
around a courtyard. This large inner
garden can only be reached from
a few gateways; the garden is really
only intended for the residents.
At the Realengracht the new housing
complex joins up with a warehouse
12.5 metres deep. It is also connected to existing buildings on the
Vierwindenstraat. The façades appear
to undulate and the effect is one of
variation.

542 centre ■

Haarlemmer Houttuinen
R. Uytenhaak
1989

A motorway was once planned here,
but the fight for housing has been
won by the neighbourhood. This
housing complex, with its 93 dwellings and an underground car park, is
situated alongside the railway, close
to Central Station. The noise from the
trains and cars made it necessary to
build an acoustic screen. Uytenhaak
therefore designed a mock façade on
the north side of the complex in order
to dampen the sound of the traffic.
The 'head' of the building is higher
and seems to suggest a ship.

543 centre ■

Rokin 99
M. van Schijndel
1990 Oudhof

A greenish-blue tympanum of ano-
dized aluminium crowns the façade
of this postmodern' office block. It
reflects vaguely the triangular roof of
the neighbouring block, but is more
a reference to Italian architecture.
The granite, in red-brown, white and
green, comes from Baveno, near Lake
Maggiore. The door handles are in
the form of two snakes, a reference
to the staff of Mercury, the god of
trade, and therefore to those using
this office block: stockbrokers.

544 centre ■

The 1990s – New Millennium

Early 1990s

The early 1990s were in many respects an elaboration of the 1980s. Dutch, and thus Amsterdam, architecture generally continued along the lines of the modern tradition. The influence of movements like post-modernism was limited to 'incidents' such as Mart van Schijndel's 'Oudhof' office building, the houses on Kerkstraat by Sjoerd Soeters, and the housing complex 'De Liefde' by Charles Vandenhove.

In a few other respects, however, the architecture of the 1990s distinguished itself from that of previous decades. The frequent use of contrasting materials in façades is typical.

For instance, in his design for Byzantium, an office and residential complex near Leidseplein, Rem Koolhaas combined a dark grey façade with a protruding golden 'oriel' at the top of the building, and Renzo Piano clad the curving volume of NEMO with oxidised copper and the ground floor with red brick.

More and more buildings were being given façades consisting of different elements which shift in relation to one another. As a result, the buildings's 'skin' seems to be detached from the rest. Good examples of this can be seen in the work of Rudy Uytenhaak and Köther & Salman. Because of the acute shortage of housing in Amsterdam, the emphasis in new building continued to be on housing. The demand for dwellings meant that most free locations, both those that became available in the city and those resulting from the city's expansion on the periphery, were earmarked for housing development. Examples of new housing development in the 1990s are the Werfterrein (completed by Lafour & Wijk), the Oranje Nassaukazerneterrein (Atelier Pro), Koningin Wilhelminaplein (Rudy Uytenhaak, De Architekten Cie.) and the GWL-terrein (Kees Christiaanse Architects & Planners).

A significant housing-development project on Amsterdam's periphery was Nieuw Sloten. The starting point here was the need for high-density, low-rise housing. Within the framework of the urban design plan for Nieuw Sloten a large number of different architects designed housing for the area (including Rudy Uytenhaak, Sjoerd Soeters, Atelier Pro, Duinker & Van der Torre, Ben Loerakker, Koen van Velsen, Lafour & Wijk and Hans Ruijssenaars). Because so many architects experimented with different types of housing, a sort of housing showroom was created. After Nieuw Sloten, the adjoining Akerpolder was also built up. Although here too single-family dwellings were amply represented, an attempt was made to realise a more urban character through the combination of high and low-rise structures and a mixture of functions. The combination building by Tangram is a good example of an urban residential block.

Another location on the periphery where large-scale housing development is under way is the Eastern Docklands. An enormous number of dwellings are being built here, to designs by various architects. The urban design plan for

KNSM Island envisaged the construction of various superblocks; the superblock had once again become an important element in urban design. Read more about this in the following chapter.

The small infills in the city are the very opposite of these housing superblocks. Even after the large-scale urban-renewal projects in Amsterdam's inner city in the 1970s and '80s, there were still small locations left undeveloped. The plots are usually so small that developing them is not commercially viable for investors; it is for individuals however. Examples of these modest contributions to the city's urban renewal can be found in the infills by Hans Wagner in Vinkenstraat and Johan Nust on Recht Boomssloot and the houses by Claus en Kaan on the Hoogte Kadijk.

Office building in Amsterdam was given renewed impetus with the realisation of office buildings in the city centre (Stadhouderskade 84, by Hans van Heeswijk) and offices near important infrastructural and economic intersections such as Schiphol and Station Zuid/WTC.

A relatively new phenomenon in the 1990s was the high-rise. High-rise structures were increasingly used to provide urban beacons in residential districts: the 'Skydome' tower on KNSM Island (to a design by Wiel Arets) and the towers in the Aker (Tangram Architecten) and Nieuw Sloten (Atelier Pro) extension districts are examples. Major projects were realized on the periphery of the city too, with very little contentious opposition. One example is the new Arena Stadium in Amsterdam-Zuidoost. It was not until the roof trusses were added that it became clear how high the structure would be and thus how much the stadium would influence the urban skyline. An even clearer example is the Rembrandt Tower by ZZDP Architects and Skidmore, Owings and Merrill (now flanked by the Breitner and Mondriaan Towers). At 135 metres this office block (completed in 1994) is the tallest building in the city. There was virtually no discussion about its height, despite the fact it can be seen from almost anywhere in the city. Perhaps this was partly because he decision-making process in relation to Rembrandt Tower coincided with a heated debate on plans for Larmag Tower. This 200-metre high tower was planned for Sloterdijk, but it will never be built.

In Amsterdam it is increasingly evident that it is necessary to make a choice between preserving monuments, or, for financial reasons, modifying them, perhaps in a far-reaching way. This issue flared up in 1994, for example, when the remains of a medieval castle were found at Nieuwezijds Kolk. Preserving these remains and making them accessible to the public was incompatible with plans to construct an office block and underground car park.

Late 1990s-2003

The second half of the 1990s witnessed not only an enormous crop of buildings, but also remarkable variation and creativity in Amsterdam architecture. This was in part a consequence of the flourishing economy and the optimism that went with it. This revival is particularly visible in residential building, not only in the construction of spectacular projects such as the Oklahoma residential complex by MVRDV or the Aquartis by Liesbeth van der Pol near the Entrepot Dock, but also in the use of materials and treatment of the façades. For instance, Erick van Egeraat covered the Tropenpunt apartment building to a great extent in stone and plates of aluminium, and Baneke and Van der Hoeven used zinc for the façade of their residential complex on the Koningin Wilhelminaplein. The windows of both complexes have been given wooden frames, which gives the dwellings a chic aura. The building on the Silodam by MVRDV proves that spectacular effects can also be achieved with inexpensive materials. The variety of dwellings that has been realised internally is reflected on the exterior by a pattern of colourful façade surfaces of corrugated sheets and panels. The complex reminds one of a container ship tied up at the quay.

Prosperity has also had its effects on the housing market. Demand among the better-off for larger, more expensive dwellings in Amsterdam is great, and their construction should initiate a trickle-down effect so that starters in the housing market also have a chance. It is striking that even within the city limits there are still areas to be found for more intensive residential use. Examples of this can be found in the Nieuwe Kerkstraat (Herder & Van der Neut), along Oosterpark (Van Sambeek & Van Veen) and on Kortenaerplein (Marlies Rohmer). These are modern buildings which are carefully integrated with the surrounding structures, so that the new construction is woven in seamlessly into the existing fabric.

Simultaneously, the second half of the 1990s saw a historicising trend here, just as in the rest of The Netherlands. Krier and Kohl built the residential complex De Meander on the Kostverlorenvaart, and the residential neighbourhood De Noorderhof near the Sloterplas. With their traditional architecture and their inward-oriented structure, they appeal to the need of residents for a familiar and intimate environment.

This period was also characterised by another trend, namely that of rising consciousness of the pressure on the environment. Among the ways this expressed itself was in the use of long-lasting, environmentally friendly materials and energy-saving measures. For example, the restaurant in the Artis Zoo (Onno Vlaanderen) is completely constructed of natural materials such as brick, wood and concrete, all of which are left untreated. The Westerpark neighbourhood saw an ecological, auto-restricted residential project, built from plans by Kees Christiaanse, which is characterised by the integration of natural elements such as watercourses and small gardens and the use of durable materials in the architecture.

Attention for energy-saving measures sometimes leads to interesting solutions, even in buildings where at first sight this concern does not appear to be so obviously present. This is the case, for instance, in the ultra-modern office building that Meyer & Van Schooten built for the ING Group on the A10 ring road. Here the space between the two layers of a double glass skin forms a buffer through which warmth can be stored in the ground, and with which the interior can be ventilated naturally. With its unusual form, the building also fulfils an important wish on the part of the client – namely that the firm receives clear recognisability by means of the architecture. The office by Steven Holl for Het Oosten Housing Corporation, with its copper-green façade, also fulfils a similar logo function. Both are examples of the renewed attention both architects and clients are giving to the office building. This development is also visible in the Teleport business park near Sloterdijk Station, and near the new ArenA Stadium. Here a new urban centre for Amsterdam Zuidoost is under construction, with various entertainment facilities and shopping malls. High office towers are rising around this core, changing Amsterdam's skyline for good. In 2007 the new metro and tram station, designed by Grimshaw & Partners, was opened. Important projects elsewhere in the city are also attracting architects of international standing. For instance, the Japanese architect Kisho Kurokawa designed the new wing of the Van Gogh Museum, and the Spanish architects Cruz & Ortiz were called upon for the renovation and expansion of the Rijksmuseum.

Around the transportation junction near the Zuid/WTC railway station, in coming decades work will be ongoing for the Zuidas, an urban area where large-scale office and residential buildings are to be combined with shopping and recreational facilities. The favourable location of the area is important: close to Schiphol and the A10 ring road. The ABN/AMRO Bank tower (Pei Cobb Freed & Partners) was the first stimulus for the development of the Zuidas, and was delivered in 1999. Recently Mahler 4 was delivered, a large office complex on which various architects will cooperate, among them Rafael Viñoly, Toyo Ito, Skidmore, Owings & Merill, Michael Graves and Medic & Puljiz (de Architekten Cie.). With its groove containing stairs, the Viñoly tower is one of the attention-getters in the complex. The whole area is expected to be finished around 2025. The construction of the Noord-/Zuidlijn, a Metro connection which will create a very fast link with Amsterdam North, Central Station, the Zuidas and Schiphol, is also important for the location. The construction of this Metro line will have major consequences for Amsterdam North too, in that it will do away with not only the physical, but also the largely psychological barrier of the IJ. The region will be tied to the rest of the city, and therefore can count on a great impulse for development.

The plans made over the past decades for the development of the southern bank of the IJ are literally at right angles to this North/South development. These plans include a chain of eight islands that were once constructed for mooring ships, railway yards, and the loading and unloading of ships and storage in warehouses. The area lost these functions many years ago, but now offers magnificent locations for future residences and workplaces. The first residential neighbourhood realised as part of the Eastern Docklands area shows that Amsterdam has rediscovered its originally so important relation with the water and over the coming decades will give it important new meaning.

Stadhouderskade
OMA (Rem Koolhaas)
1991 Byzantium

A number of prestigious projects have been realized near the Leidseplein. OMA designed Byzantium; the tower block of the complex accommodates offices and luxury apartments in the sober light-grey blocks. The golden 'bon-bon box' is also an apartment. Opposite Byzantium is the Casino, with its marble walls and glass awnings. Hans Ruijssenaars is the architect. The shops and flats next to the Casino are by Kees Spanjers and Pieter Zaanen. The new building is combined with parts of the old prison complex.

601 centre ■

Stadhouderskade 84
Hans van Heeswijk
1991 office

By using concrete, steel and glass in the design of this office building, which is adjacent to the Geïllustreerde Pers (see 507), a deliberate contrast has been sought with the largely brick-built development of the surrounding area. The building has a curtain wall. The glass lift tower is thirty metres high. There is a two-storey entrance which leads to a reception area situated in a light court. The entire ground floor is given over to office spaces, which are arranged around a patio.

602 centre ■

Tweede Bloemdwarsstraat
Cees Nagelkerke
1991 housing

The dwellings are characterized by metal pergolas that hang above the narrow street (hence the project's nickname, the 'hanging gardens'). The pergolas are part of the balconies of the top-floor dwellings. Nagelkerke designed a series of infills in different locations in the Jordaan. Together they provided forty-three dwellings and three commercial premises.

603 centre ■

Sarphatistraat 470
Koen van Velsen
1992 Rijksakademie

Koen van Velsen converted the former cavalry barracks and stables into a home for the Academy of Fine Arts. He took 'meeting' as his point of departure, and transparency and sight lines are therefore central to his design. Two new buildings have been erected in the inner courtyard: a central building (providing, among other things, the main entrance, exhibition space, and offices) and a tower containing a library and media information centre. The new buildings are linked to the barracks by four transparent elevated walkways.

604 tram 9, 10, 14 □

Da Costakade
Charles Vandenhove
1992 De Liefde

The most important projects of the
Belgian architect Charles Vandenhove
are situated in urban-renewal locations in Oud-West. The housing
complex 'De Liefde' is built on the
site of a church of the same name
designed by P.J.H. Cuypers. The
building is characterized by postmodern elements such as tympani and
neck-gables.
It also has concrete decorative elements and round arches above the
recessed balconies.

605 tram 3, 7, 12, 13, 14, 17 ☐

Sarphatistraat
Atelier PRO
1992 Housing

Atelier PRO designed more than 300
dwellings on the site of the Oranje
Nassaukazerne. They invited six foreign architects each to design a residential tower along the water. Those
invited were (from west to east) Koji
Yagi (Japan), Alexandros Tombazis
(Greece), Cuno Brullmann (France),
Patrick Pinnell (USA), Tage Lyneborg
(Sweden) and Jeremy Bailey (Great
Britain). Their designs were subsequently elaborated by Atelier PRO,
who also provided the detailing.

606 tram 7, 9, 14 ■

Plantage Middenlaan 2
Zwarts & Jansma architects
1993 Hortus Botanicus

Amsterdam's old Hortus was enlarged in 1993 with the addition of a hot-house consisting of three separate glass-houses, each with a different climate. A walkway allows one to walk through the tops of the palms. Construction costs were kept low by using standard green-house-construction elements. In order to allow as much sunlight as possible to penetrate, these elements are sus-pended from a loadbearing structure that determines the appearance of the hothouse.

607 tram 9, 14 ☐

Schiphol Airport
Benthem Crouwel
1993-2004

Schiphol was provided with a new terminal, Terminal 3, as part of a largescale plan to the entire airport area. In the design Jan Benthem has adopted the same ideas that char-acterized the existing terminals (M. Duintjer, 1967-1971), resulting in a building with a clear structure, neutral in colour. The new terminal is constructed largely from glass and steel. The building adjoins Schiphol Plaza, which is both railway station and shopping centre.

608 trains ☐

Oosterdok
Renzo Piano
1994-1997 NEMO

The NEMO, the National Centre for
Science and Technology, is constructed in
the Oosterdok as a link between the city
centre and the IJ. The museum is build
at the southern entrance to the IJtunnel,
close to the Scheepvaartmuseum (see
152), and provide access from Central
Station along the Langedoksbrug (Henk
Meijer, 1992). The Italian architect Renzo
Piano has designed a museum with a
total surface area of more than 11,000
m^2. Its curved volume is clad with oxidized
copper plates, with their green colour.
From the urban square at the roof a great
panoramic view is created over city and IJ.

609 centre ☐

Gustav Mahlerlaan
Pei Cobb Freed & Partners
1994-1999 Headquarters
ABN AMRO Bank

The American architectural firm Pei Cobb
Freed & Partners won the competition
to design a new headquarters for the
ABN AMRO Bank. The prestigious building is situated near the ringway and
railway station Zuid/WTC, as part of the
development of the city's Zuidas. Henry
Cobb designed a complex consisting of a
number of elements: a low-rise building
with offices and a non-public banking
space, a 105 metres high office tower on
a large forecourt, and a separate confer-
ence centre.

610 tram 5, metro 51, trains ■

Amsterdam-Zuidoost
Grabowski & Poort
1996 Amsterdam Arena

Amsterdam Arena is home to Ajax football club. The design (for which Sjoerd Soeters is aestethic adviser) has a roof which can be opened and closed, allowing the stadium to be used even in poor weather. The Arena is also suitable for major events such as concerts. With the arrival of the stadium and the construction close by of shops, a concert hall and cinema complex (Frits van Dongen, de Architekten Cie). The previously dull office area has become much more lively.

611 metro, trains Bijlmer □

Bijlmerdreef
Claus en Kaan
1997

As part of the renewal operation in the Bijlmer the central traffic artery was lowered and transformed into a green boulevard. With the lowering the separation of functions, which was so much a mark of this high-rise area, definitively disappeared from the scene. Low-rise structures have been realised on both sides, with four-storey high residential buildings bordering the Bijlmerdreef itself. The stacked upper and lower dwellings each have their front doors at street level.

612 metro 50, 54, bus 59, 60 ■

Ookmeerweg, Reimerswaalstraat
MVRDV
1997 Oklahoma

This complex in the Western Garden
Cities contains 21 different types of
dwellings for senior citizens. In order
to obtain the intended 100 dwellings in the block, MVRDV permitted
thirteen dwellings, as deep as the flat
itself, to protrude from the building.
A steel construction makes the incon-
ceivable possible. The pendent dwellings, clad with cedar wood, stand
out against the predominately glass
façade. The other side of the block
consists of a wooden façade that is
defined by a playful pattern of balconies clad with coloured Plexiglas.

613 tram 1, 17, bus 23 ■

Nieuw-Gerenstein
Claus en Kaan
1998 Transitional dwellings

The architects have introduced a new
dwelling type between the existing
urban structure and a new neighbourhood with single-family residences. In
the transition zone between the existing high-rise flats and the new low-rise
structures they have placed twelve towers which serve as 'transitional inserts'.
Four dwellings, divided over two aisles,
lie on each storey. By displacing the
aisles with regard to one another, not
only do the towers appear slimmer, but
an extra façade surface is created that
provides extra light. The dwellings differ
in depth, permitting the realisation of
different types of residences.

614 metro 50, 54, bus 59, 60 ■

Hoogte Kadijk
Claus en Kaan
1998

Claus & Kaan realised two plots with socially subsidised rental dwellings on either side of the Hoogte Kadijk. In order to make the small houses as flexible as possible they used open floor plans. The storage areas, which often claim a part of the street side façade, are moved to the rear, strengthening the relation between the dwellings and the street. The front façades are characterised by a strong relief. The combinations of red brick and window openings, which consist of a deep-lying window with a heavily framed transom, remind one of the architecture of old Dutch houses.

615 bus 22, tram 9, 14 ■

Buyskade, Donker Curtiusstraat
Van der Waals/Zeinstra
1998 Dwellings and business spaces

The combination of living and work functions was the point of departure for this project. Slim, brick clad three-storey high residential buildings have been placed along the water. On the street side glass stairwells thrust forward on steel columns. The wooden dwellings with lectern roofs situated between the towers are striking. Work spaces have been created in these dwellings and the recessed bases of the towers. Behind the project, lies a second U-shaped residential complex that forms a transition with the closed blocks in the neighbourhood.

616 bus 18, tram 3 ■

Oosterpark
Van Sambeek & Van Veen
1998

The designers sought to connect with the allure of the adjoining row of majestic 19th century façades. The façade is classically ordered, with a plinth, portico, brick skin and cornice. The dark bricks are laid in a vertical bond and the window frames are made as narrow as possible, creating a taut skin for the façade. Financial considerations required the building of five residential layers rather than the usual four. By enlarging the window and door openings on the bottom the project blends into the street wall harmoniously without losing its individuality.

617 bus 37, tram 7, 10 ■

Kortenaerplein, Slatuinenweg
Marlies Rohmer
1998

The project is divided into two parts: two apartment blocks on a triangular plaza and two rows of houses on a quiet adjoining street. In terms of size and scale the five-storey high apartment blocks blend in with the Amsterdam School blocks behind them, and offer views of the Kostverlorenkade. The dwellings have entrances on the plaza or from a gallery on the third storey. The single-family homes (photo) fill holes in an old street and are characterised by their large wooden roof overhangs, reminiscent of monks' cowls.

618 tram 12, 13, 14 ■

Haarlemmerweg
Kees Christiaanse
1998 former GWL terrein

An environmentally friendly and auto-restricted residential neighbourhood has been realised on this former municipal water department site. In addition to the urban development plan, Christiaanse also designed three residential blocks, including the nine-storey high apartment building that borders the north side of the area. The north façade, on the Haarlemmerweg, has a closed quality, while the south façade is comprised of glass and balconies. The ecological aspect comes to the fore in the use of sustainable materials, the orientation of the dwellings to the sun, and the collection and reuse of rain water.

619 tram 10, bus 21 ■

Oeverpad
De Architektengroep (Dick van Gameren, Bjarne Mastenbroek)
1998 Residences and residential care complex

This residential care complex for senior citizens, combined with rental and owner-occupied dwellings, consists of a U-shaped structure on a half-sunken parking garage. The southern leg is low, to permit as much sun to enter as possible. The building embraces a garden from which, via a gate, there are views of the Sloterplas. Using inexpensive materials such as brick, corrugated aluminium and steel fencing left budgetary space for introducing special details at other points: wood window frames and sliding windows.

620 bus 19, 63 ■

Sloterkade
Köther & Salman
1999 'Lightfactory'

Köther & Salman designed this
complex for a former factory site,
with dwellings grouped into a factory
building that was retained and into
a new block, the top two storeys
of which project over the factory.
There is a great diversity of types of
dwellings. Particularly in the factory
building there are very spacious loft
dwellings, sometimes as much as
four metres high. In the new building
voids, extra storeys and depths have
been used. The front façade consists
of a light skin of glass and aluminium
and a screen of wood slats.

621 tram 2 ■

Plantage Middenlaan
Onno Vlaanderen Architects
1999 Restaurant, Artis Zoo

The restaurant stands on a small strip
of water on the one side to the new
animal enclosures and on the other
to the historic warehouses across the
water. The building comprises a high,
elongated glass structure. A whimsical volume of masonry is thrust into
this, in which the kitchen and sanitary
facilities are collected. The floors are
connected with ramps and stairs that
wind through the space like mountain
paths and constantly provide new perspectives. The glass façade is articulated by vertical wooden uprights.

622 tram 9, 14 □

Koningin Wilhelminaplein
Baneke Van der Hoeven
Architects
1999

This residential block borders on a plaza and a park lying behind it. The building stands on a plinth of two storeys, with a parking garage on the ground floor and dwellings on the first storey that stretch back the full depth. A zigzag six-storey building stands on the dark grey plinth. The façade facing the park is open in character. On the street side the façade is clad with zinc and shiny glass sheets. This urban wall has vertical accents at the staircases.

623 tram 2 ■

Iseoplantsoen and vicinity
Diederen, Dirrix, Van Wylick
1999

In the middle of the newly constructed neighbourhood De Aker lies the grand Iseoplantsoen with its small lake. The architects designed houses that present themselves as a series of linked two-family residences. The dwellings are characterised by a projecting element in which the open kitchen lies. The living room is situated at the back. The façades of the dwellings are comprised chiefly of white brick. The projecting element is clad in western red cedar. A steel canopy provides a visual horizontal link between the houses.

624 tram 1 ■

Polderweg
Architects Studio Herman
Hertzberger
1999 Montessori College

About 1000 pupils of 56 nationalities
attend this school. Hertzberger wanted
to create a complex which calls up
associations with the city and street,
where young people would want to hang
around. The ground plan consists of a
V-shape in which the classrooms are
grouped in the long leg parallel to the
road, and the workshops and gymnasium in the leg behind it. In the point
of the V is a spacious, high auditorium.
Considerable attention has been devoted
to informal places for sitting and study.

625 tram 9 ■

Burgemeester Roëlstraat,
Slotermeerlaan
Rob Krier, Mark Tuerlings, Joris Deur
1999 Noorderhof

The new neighbourhood of Noorderhof
lies in the Western Garden Cities. An old
church has been retained as the centre
for the new complex. The isolated location is utilised to construct an introverted
residential neighbourhood with high-rise
on the edges and the intimacy of a vil-
lage in the internal streets. The high-rise
rim includes gatehouses which remind
one of medieval city gates. This concept
is in sharp contrast to the original open
and spacious character of the Western
Garden Cities. The street scene is made
as varied as possible.

626 tram 13 ■

Eurokade, Valutaboulevard
Heren 5
1999 Crescent

At the centre of the new neighbourhood De Aker lies the Ecuplein. The block comprises single-family homes: four-storey dwellings of narrow width. Continuous window strips provide horizontality in the façade. These strips become narrower the higher they are on the building. The façades are finished in a dark purple glossy brick. There is always a cleft cut away in the masonry between the dwellings to emphasise the individuality of each house.

627 tram 1 ■

Pieter Calandlaan
Tangram
1999 'Zorro'

At the intersection of the two main axes, Pieter Calandlaan and De Alpen, lies this 18-storey residential tower. The architecture of this building underlines its key role by a dynamic façade that seems to suggest a swirling movement. From the 17th storey the windows wrap around the tower in a downward spiral. Dark grey sheeting and orange fields accompany this screw thread. As a result of the unusual floor plan of the building, every dwelling has good exposure to the sun.

628 tram 1 ■

Paulus Potterstraat 7
Kisho Kurokawa, in cooperation
with Greiner Van Goor Architecten
1999 New Wing, Van Gogh
Museum

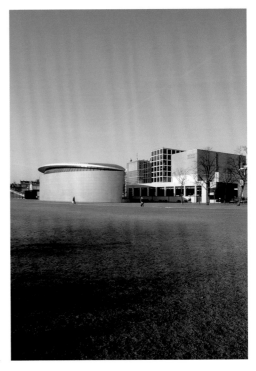

Escalators under Museumplein connect the new section with the main
building by Gerrit Rietveld. To avoid
blocking a number of sight lines
in Museumplein, the free-standing
building has an elliptical floor plan.
The one half of the ellipse is a volume with three levels of exhibition
spaces. The other half includes a
sunken patio around which a curved
exhibition corridor runs. Strips of windows between the roof and the grey
stone walls provide for natural light.

629 centre ☐

Prinsengracht 267
Benthem Crouwel Architecten
1999 Extension, Anne Frank
House

The old canal house has been
extended with a new museum building in order to absorb the pressure of
its many visitors. All the museal
facilities are grouped in the new
wing, permitting the interior of the old
house to be reconstructed as it was
in Anne Frank's time. The entrance
and exit are widely separated so that
the stream of visitors is kept separate
and the flow through runs smoothly.
Associations with the surrounding old
houses are sought in the façade, in
order to express the threefold function
of the building.

630 centre ☐

Sarphatistraat, Singelgracht
Steven Holl, 2000 Headquarters,
Het Oosten Housing Corporation

A pavilion that can be used as meeting space and an employees' restaurant has been added to the Singelgracht side of an existing complex. To a great extent the interior consists of open space, into which two balconies protrude. Outside, a façade of perforated copper sheeting with large openings has been placed in front of the actual façade. A second perforated wall is placed in front of the façade on the inside, here and there running in front of the windows. Brightly coloured areas are introduced onto the middle wall. The perforations and reflections create a play of colours in three dimensions.

631 tram 9, 14 ∎

Nieuwe Kerkstraat
HVDN Architecten
2000

This new building forms a careful transition from the small scale of the 17th century Nieuwe Kerkstraat to the large scale of the Weesperstraat. The wall is divided into two sections, separated by a narrow areaway with steps. The horizontally articulated block abuts the Weesperstraat and contains residences for senior citizens, with shops on the ground floor. The other block follows the structure of the Nieuwe Kerkstraat, shifting to a more horizontal articulation. The combination living/working premises on the lowest layer are recognisable by their high glass 'shop fronts'.

632 metro 50 Weesperplein ∎

Van der Palmkade
Krier & Kohl
2000 De Meander

The name of this apartment complex refers to the building's meandering ground plan. In the design, on the one hand it was the intention to realise as many dwellings as possible on the limited number of square meters and on the other to also leave public space for recreational purposes. The complex is built in an historicising architecture with plenty of brick and ornamentation on the façade. Yet, with the ground plan and round corner towers, the conscious decision was made not to link the architecture with that of the surrounding 19th century buildings.

633 tram 3 ☐

Entrepotdok
Zeinstra Van der Pol
2001 Aquartis

Aquartis is located in an area with warehouses rebuilt as dwellings and stands on the site of a former coal yard, one massive wall of which has been integrated into the front façade. The façade rises in steps, making it reminiscent of factory architecture.
The building comprises 110 owner-occupied dwellings of diverse types, varying from artist's studios below to penthouses with views over the adjoining zoo at the top. All the dwellings have a southern exposure and possess a conservatory that is separated from the living space by a glass wall.

634 tram 10 ■

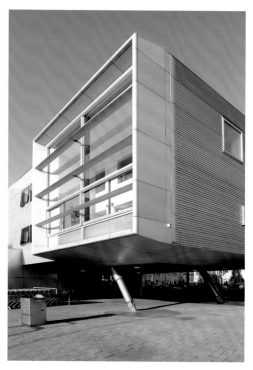

Cornelis Outshoornstraat
Venhoeven CS
2001 U2 Geuzenveld

The U2 residential complex is exemplary of the demolition/new construction projects that are part of the renewal of the Western Garden Cities. The complex comprises 130 subsidised rental units, owner occupied properties, residences for the handicapped, psychiatric residential care facilities for the elderly and shops. The complexity of this assignment is reflected in the ingenious combinations of entries. The exterior is on the other hand characterised by simplicity in the glass façade with its aluminium window frames placed flush in the façade.

635 bus 21 ■

Stadhouderskade
Cruz y Ortiz
2001 (design) New construction and restoration, Rijksmuseum

Three important elements in the design are the breaking open of three light wells, maintaining the bicycle route through the central gate of the building, and moving the entrance to this underpass. From this passage, via escalators one will reach a space that connects the east and west entry halls with one another. The entrance to the exhibitions is planned in the west light courtyard, a shop and cafe in the east. In the restoration of the building the architectural concept of P.J.H. Cuypers will be reinstated as much as possible.

636 centre □

Stationsplein
VMX Architects
2001 Bicycle flat

Built as a temporary accommodation
for 2500 bicycles, the three-storey
'bicycle flat' is still in use, despite
the city's intention to tow the structure away from its present location.
Perhaps the fascination which foreign
tourists have shown for this floating
'parking garage' for bicycles has led
the city to misgivings about its intention, which was declared as far back
as 2004. Thanks to the sloping steel
construction one can bicycle up and
down through the flat; the complaint
however is that it is almost impossible
to find your bicycle again.

637 tram 1, 2, 5, 13, 17 ■

Silodam
MVRDV
2002

This residential complex is sited in
an impressive location on the IJ,
next door to two former grain eleva-
tors (both renovated by A.J. & J. van
Stigt). Several communal facilities
and a collective terrace on the water
are accessible from ground level.
The diverse types of residences
are grouped and stacked on one
another. By connecting the groups by
internal streets, MVRDV has created
a microcosmos which is reflected in
the exterior. The colourful fields in
the façade remind one of a container
ship tied up at the quayside.

638 centre ■

Mauritskade, Von Zesenstraat
Erick van Egeraat Associated Architects
2002 Tropenpunt

Tropenpunt is opposite the Tropical Museum in the Dapperbuurt. The building ties together two 19th century residential blocks, creating a new crown for the corner. While the building first follows the vertical articulation of the existing residential blocks, toward the point this shifts to a horizontal division in which the windows become steadily higher as they near the angle. The rounded-off angle forms the climax of the project. Here the building is high, transparent and slopes obliquely toward the bottom.

639 tram 9, 14 ■

Amstelveenseweg 500
Meyer & Van Schooten
2002 ING House

The headquarters of the ING Group is part of the Zuidas, a new office and residential area surrounding an important transportation junction between Zuid/WTC and the airport. This advantageous location in part defines the important logo function of the building. The building stands on high legs giving many spaces splendid views. The interior is characterised by a large number of atria, loggias and indoor gardens. Considerable attention has been devoted to energy management. The space in the double façade works as a buffer and is ventilated naturally.

640 tram 16, 24, metro 50 ■

Nieuwe Foelistraat
Verburg Hoogendijk Architecten
2002 Supermarket

While awaiting the new layout of the street between the Mr. Visserplein and the IJ Tunnel, a temporary building has been realised near the tunnel on a vacant lot. The construction was created after a supermarket had spotted the site and saw the possibilities for a temporary expansion. The cafe is located on the ground floor and combined with business space above. Because of the presence of underground cables and mains the structure had to be extremely light. The construction consists of steel panels which are spanned by a plastic roof.

641 centre ☐

Prins Hendrikkade
René van Zuuk
2003 ARCAM, Architecture Centre
Amsterdam

In monumental surroundings Van Zuuk designed a compact, sculptural building with three layers: an exhibition space on the level of the Prins Hendrikkade, with above it office space and beneath it, on the water, a multi-functional space where meetings and discussions can take place. The full height and width of the façade on the west side consists of glass. Further, the structure is clad with silvery calzip that is folded around the building, over the roof and down to the ground on the quay side. The sculptural form of the entrance on this side is exceptional.

642 centre ☐

Strawinksylaan, World Trade Centre
G. de Klerk/P. Selle 1985
Renovation and new construction
2002-2003 by KPF and Van den
Oever, Zaaijer and Partners

The large, blue, light-reflecting office complex by G. de Klerk and P. Selle has been entirely replaced and expanded since 2003 by Kohn Pedersen Fox and Van den Oever, Zaaijer and Partners. In place of the reflecting glass has come a double façade of clear glass with terracotta painted louvre panels used behind it. In addition to the new towers several generous awnings, among other things, have been added to the extension as connecting elements.

643 metro 50, 51, tram 5 ☐

Oosterdoks Iland
Erick van Egeraat Associated
Architects
2000 design

The southern bank of the IJ consists of a necklace of islands along the IJ, on both sides of Central Station. Over a period of fifteen years these islands will be renewed one by one. The urban development plan by Erick van Egeraat for Oosterdoks Island is based on six plots which will be separated from one another by a fan-like street pattern. The height of the buildings will vary from 24 metres to 47 metres. Various international architects are collaborating to fill in the plans for the island, including Baumschlager-Eberle-Grassbaum, Future Systems, Cruz y Ortiz and Toyo Ito.

644 centre

Westerdoks Iland
Peter Defesche (OD205)
(urban development plan)
2000 design

According to the master plan by Peter
Defesche (OD205) an urban residential
neighbourhood should be developed on
Westerdoks Island, with a mix of dwellings, commercial spaces and facilities.
The structures on the city side of the
island should connect with the compact
brick city centre and will consist of four
large blocks around inner courts. On the IJ
side the structures will reflect the vastness
of the water and follow the series of large
buildings on the IJ. A harbour with quays
will link the city and IJ sides.

645 centre

Gustav Mahlerlaan and vicinity - Zuidas
De Architekten Cie. - Branimir Medic
and Pero Puljiz (urban development
plan)
2002-2007 Mahler 4

Mahler 4 is a component of the Zuidas
and consists of nine buildings which are
connected to one another by a plinth two
layers high in which public facilities are
situated. Primarily offices will be realised
in the outer blocks of buildings; the central tower will be residential. The project
started in 2002, with the office buildings
by Rafael Viñoly, Michael Graves and
SOM and the residential tower by Toyo Ito.
The final phase has started in 2004 with
designs by Foreign Office Architects, EEA
- Erick van Egeraat Associated Architects,
Bosch Architects and UN Studio.

646 metro 50 ■

Building on islands

The Eastern Docklands

Over the past decade Amsterdam's Eastern Docklands has been built up with about 8,000 dwellings, stores, businesses, schools and various recreational facilities. Hardly was the area finished and it was already attracting countless architectural tourists from here and far to admire this colourful collection of innovative architecture and urban planning experiments. The area consists of artificial islands and peninsulas which were constructed between 1874 and 1927 to meet the needs of Amsterdam's flourishing harbour. Commodities arrived on large modern steamships and were unloaded into the warehouses and sheds on shore, to then be distributed from there by land. By the 1970s however the area lost its function, in part as a consequence of the removal of the port facilities to the Western Harbours, and the area fell into decay. For a long time nothing happened, until in 1975 the City Council decided to realise a residential neighbourhood in the Eastern Docklands, with the very high density of an average of 100 dwellings per hectare, in contrast to the usual 30 dwellings per hectare.

The definitive course was defined for the development of this archipelago in 1990. It was decided to keep the harbour mouths open and to take the form of the peninsulas as the point of departure. Views over the water played a large role in this. It was also decided that the water should take over the role of green spaces in landlocked development. On each island these principles would be interpreted differently and worked out by various urban planners, giving each island or peninsula its own character. The overarching direction lay in the hands of urban planner Ton Schaap, of Amsterdam's Municipal Urban Planning Department (DRO). Because the redevelopment of the whole area took place over a period of more than 25 years, the area reflects changes in the field of urban planning, architecture and housing in The Netherlands.

Abattoir and Cattle Market sites and Entrepot-West

A start was made in the late 1980s with the rebuilding of the former Abattoir and Cattle Market sites and Entrepot-West, the region to the west of the Entrepot Harbour. While the plans for the Abattoir and Cattle Market sites were still characterised by government subsidised rental housing in a somewhat dated pattern of low-rise apartment blocks in the midst of green, in the neighbourhoods developed after that there was abundant experimentation with new models for subdividing the sites.

With the development of Entrepot-West, the idea of apartment blocks grouped around a cul-de-sac was abandoned, and a search began for a more urban concept of lot division and buildings that was suitable for the situation. As part of a multiple study commission a design by the DRO for a square building block was worked out by Atelier Pro into a half-open lot division with both low-rise structures and high-rise accents. It is characterised by a mix of rental and owner-occupied housing, and the increased attention on the part of planners and designers for variation in what was to be built.

KNSM Island

After the decision had been made to design the area north of the Abattoir and Cattle Market sites and Entrepot-West as a archipelago, keeping the old harbour mouths open, various architects and urban planners were brought in to fill in this general proposal for the new neighbourhood on the basis of the DRO's regional sketches. The following period was used to seek solutions for the high residential density in a limited area, combined with the search for more variation in residential neighbourhoods that was fashionable everywhere in The Netherlands. A choice was made to realise a substantial number of more expensive dwellings (primarily owner-occupied) in order to stem the outflow of wealthier Amsterdammers to other areas.

On the KNSM Island these ambitions took shape in a master plan by Jo Coenen. Coenen opted for a classic arrangement in which he took the monumental character of the area as his starting point. He divided the Island lengthwise with a wide avenue, the KNSM-laan. On either side the avenue is flanked by monumental residential blocks and a number of restored harbour buildings. On the northern quay stands the Skydome, a 20-storey high residential tower by Wiel Arets. The tower is visible from the distance, and is therefore also clearly intended as a landmark for the area. Further, four apartment blocks by the brothers Wintermans were built along this north quay. At the very tip of the Island lies the Emerald Empire by Jo Coenen himself. The circular residential structure is surrounded by a pearl necklace of villas. On the southern quay lie two 'superblocks', residential buildings 170 metres long, 60 metres wide and eight storeys high, with shops, offices and restaurants and cafes in the plinth. 'Piraeus', by Hans Kollhoff and Christian Rapp, stands on the quay like a robust sculpture. The neighbouring neo-classical structure by Bruno Albert has a round plaza in its heart, with in its southern entry an ornamental gate by Narcisse Tordoir. A third superblock is located at the point where Java Island abuts KNSM Island. This building by Diener & Diener not only functions as a gateway but as a transition between the two urban planning visions of the two islands. It comprises two separate buildings that are striking in their refusal to call attention to themselves.

Java Island

Sjoerd Soeters drew up a master plan for the long and narrow Java Island (1991). The plan differs strongly from the approach on KNSM Island. In contrast to the wide blocks of the KNSM Island, Soeters provided the island with long walls of building fronts, of high-rise residential buildings on the quays, so that most dwellings had a view of the water. The walls are comprised of buildings designed by various architects, each of which are 27 metres wide and always contain only one type of dwelling. Repeating these 'stamps' at various places on the Island has created an architectural patchwork quilt. The buildings along the quays enclose a protected inner area in which bicycle paths, gardens, small squares and repeated pairs of low-rise, freestanding residential blocks are included. It may be clear that Soeters was inspired by Amsterdam's ring canals, which are reflected in the verticality and variation of the building. He also introduced small canals which divide the island into five sections. Various young architects, the so-called 'Young Heroes', designed the small houses on these cross-canals. John Bosch and Dana Ponec used the classic design of the canal house, while Art Zaaijer realised a modern variant on the old theme.

Borneo and Sporenburg

The plan by West 8 for the Borneo and Sporenburg peninsulas is spectacular. Never before in The Netherlands were so many dwellings, each with a street-level entrance, built at such a high density. Adriaan Geuze of West 8 conceived a new plot plan for 100 dwellings per hectare. In order to obtain this density with the low-rise dwellings for families with children which were wanted by the city, the area is subdivided into rows of back-to-back houses with patios or roof terraces. This produces inward-oriented dwellings with a high degree of privacy. In relation to that, it is also important that all the houses have their own front door on the street, and that the streets are narrow, because a large amount of the parking must take place on the individual plot. The result is a sharp contrast between the enclosed privacy of the dwellings and the vast prospects over the IJ.

Working out these dwellings was in the hands of 36 architects, who on the basis of a prototype designed a large number of new kinds of patio residences with flexible room arrangements. Most dwellings have a ground floor 3.5 metres high, which affords room for intermediate storeys, galleries and, moreover, ample light penetration. In most dwellings the living space is situated on an upper storey, sharply accentuating the division between public and private space. Pre-selected materials, chiefly dark red brick, western red cedar and folding gates, provide coherence in the residential streets.

The basic conditions set down by West 8 and the Municipal Urban Planning Department forced the architects to the greatest creativity possible. The results of this are chiefly to be found behind the façades, but in some cases can also be read from the exterior, as in the wedge-shaped dwellings by Van Herk & De Kleijn, the alternately built upon and unbuilt lots of M3H and the houses by Neutelings Riedijk Architects, with their overhanging cedar boxes that afford a view of the street. The dwellings at the tips of the peninsulas have been given a quarter turn with respect to the prevailing direction of the buildings, and are also distinguished by their use of materials. Josep Lluís Mateo clad his houses with tropical hardwood, Mastenbroek and Van Gameren provided their owner-occupied homes with projecting, roofed terraces clad with variously coloured glass. In the middle of the sea of houses on Borneo-Sporenburg are three large residential structures. These appear to have fallen as 'meteorites', but in reality are very carefully positioned on sightlines at critical points in the vicinity. For instance the Pacman building by Van Velsen is placed in line with the Oranje Locks, The Whale by Frits van Dongen in line with the Verbindingsdam, and the third monolith should lie on the sight-axis of the eastern approach to the Piet Hein Tunnel, but will not be realised.

Scheepstimmermanstraat

A special experiment was carried out on Scheepstimmermanstraat on Borneo, where 60 empty lots were distributed to buyers who could have a house constructed to their own design. Both continuity and variation were qualities sought for in the street wall which would be formed by the separate façades. For this reason these 'dream houses' too were to be realised within strict basic conditions. All the lots were 16 metres deep and varied in width from 4.2 to 6 metres. The maximum height of the houses is 9.2 metre, and the ground floor had to be 3.5 metres high. Parking had to be provided for within the building. Access to the houses was from Scheepstimmermanstraat; on the back the plots border directly on the water of a mooring place. For those so minded, the narrow, deep residences on the water are reminiscent of Amsterdam's ring canals. The whole approach is also reminiscent of the 17th century, because then too clients were given considerable freedom within strict urban planning guidelines to put up houses of their own.

Most of the houses in Scheepstimmermanstraat are oriented to the back, because of their location on the water and the southern exposure. Here the façades are open, and at various points small gardens and terraces have been realised at the water's edge. The street side façades have a closed character and often literally serve as screens (see the houses by FARO and Koen van Velsen). At some points architects have come up with very surprising solutions. For instance, MVRDV built on only half a lot, creating both a narrow residence and an 'alley'. Thanks to a glass façade the house is totally oriented to the alleyway, and enjoys optimal privacy.

The results on Scheepstimmermanstraat can be seen as a reflection of the prevailing ideas in housing in the 1990s, which were to a great extent defined by the wishes of home-seekers. Although some critical notes can be made with regard to the project – for instance, the inhospitableness of the street side – both the clients and the city view the experiment as a success, and it will have a successor on Steiger Island in IJburg.

Rietlanden

The centre of the area, the 'Rietlanden', is the hinge point between the Eastern Docklands and the city centre, both in spatial terms and for transportation. Moreover, the entrance to the Piet Hein Tunnel makes the Rietlanden an important gateway to the city. The structures in this centre are a combination of old and new buildings. The 'Brazilië' shopping mall lies next to the Verbindingsdam. Opposite it lie various historic buildings from the Royal Dutch Lloyd period, including the Lloyd Hotel, which has been rebuilt by MVRDV into a hotel for artists and art lovers. Behind the hotel lies Rietland Park, where nine modern residential and office towers (Ton Venhoeven and Hans van Heeswijk) stand as separate volumes in the greenery. The southern boundary of the park is marked by the oblique upward slope of a building by Rudy Uytenhaak.

Public spaces

The attention given from the very first to the design of public spaces in the development of plans for the Eastern Docklands was striking. In each sub-section links were sought with the former maritime character of the area. Here and there old buildings from the Royal Dutch Steamship Company (KNSM), warehouses and hoisting cranes still stand, elements which were deliberately retained and integrated into the new area. Such links with the past are also sought in the use of materials. For instance, on the Java and KNSM islands old, rusty Stelcon plates were reused. Further, the street profiles are simple, and as much as possible unity has been created in the pavement of all streets, sidewalks and parking places.

In the densely built-up neighbourhoods water has taken over the visual function of green spaces. Nevertheless, interesting parks and gardens have been laid out at a number of points. For instance, on Java Island four different enclosed gardens have been constructed from designs by Jan Stigter and Ton Schaap (DRO). The gardens are arranged according to the theme of the succession of the seasons, and are all crossed by a bicycle path that runs the full length of the Island. The compact plan for Borneo and Sporenburg permitted almost no public parks, although the diagonal strip of green on Sporenburg is an exception. Through its careful positioning spectacular views are created on both sides. For the Rietlands, together with the DRO the offices of Sant & Co. designed a raised park that is cut through by bicycle paths and roads. Various recreational facilities such as tennis courts, a sloping playground for youth on the roof of the Piet Hein Tunnel, and other sports fields are to be found there. The over 200 trees that will be planted in the green space will make the Rietland Park an important orienta-tion point in the area.

IJburg Archipelago

While it can be seen that an emphatically urban area has been realised in the Eastern Docklands, which despite its initially isolated location has acquired a distinct place in Amsterdam's life, work is still ongoing on Amsterdam's largest expansion in years: IJburg. As early as 1981 the city launched plans for a new neighbourhood on the IJ to the east of Amsterdam. After a referendum in 1997 work began on the definitive plans for IJburg. A team of urban planners under the leadership of Frits Palmboom and Jaap van den Bout opted for the development of an archipelago with 18,000 dwellings for 43,000 residents, and diverse amenities such as schools, stores, commercial spaces and yacht harbours. A separate urban planing proposal would be made for each island, giving each island its own character. In order to respond to new developments, the islands will be built one at a time. The land for the first two islands, Steiger Island and Haven Island, has already been dredged up, and a causeway and two bridges (Grimshaw & Partners) now connect IJburg to the city.

Steiger Island is split into thirds by the main road to IJburg and high-tension lines. The designers of the urban development plan – Mirjana Milanovic, Pieter Klomp and Iris van der Helm (DRO) – have taken this as their starting point and emphasised the character of each subsection, creating a 'collage city'. Steiger Island will afford room for special residential forms such as floating dwellings by Marlies Rohmer and self-built homes. The urban development plan for Haven Island was drawn up by Felix Claus (Claus & Kaan Architects), Frits van Dongen (de Architekten Cie.) and Ton Schaap (DRO). The plan is based on a grid pattern of streets and closed blocks which will each be elaborated by different architects, under the guidance of a supervisor. The blocks will alternate with public spaces and internal water features. The first dwellings on Haven Island were delivered at the end of 2002.

Public transit: tram 10 and 26, bus 43.

Enneus Heerma Bridge

**Hildo Kropplein, J.M. van der
Meylaan and vicinity
Lafour & Wijk
1987-1989**

The assignment consisted of building a large number of homes on
a large, elongated site where a
slaughterhouse had previously stood.
In contrast to the U-shaped blocks
suggested by the Municipal Urban
Planning Department, Lafour & Wijk
designed an open lot plan in which
views of the water and the penetration of sunlight played a large role.
They succeeded in realising a great
diversity of dwelling types in the
pastel-coloured blocks within a limited budget.

701 bus 43 ■

**Entrepot-West
Atelier PRO
1991-1997**

The urban development plans from the
Municipal Urban Planning Department
for the redevelopment of the area
to the west of the Entrepot Harbour
provided for a large, square block
that would vault over the harbour like
a castle. Atelier PRO worked out this
idea into a half-open lot plan with
both low-rise building and high-rise
accents. The eye-catcher is the building of five storeys slung out over the
water, protecting the other buildings
from the noise of the neighbouring
railway lines. The rental and owner-
occupied properties are accommodated in various types of dwellings.

702 bus 43 ■

KNSM-laan, Barcelonaplein
Bruno Albert
1993

The building is one of the two 'super-blocks' which, according to the classic arrangement of the urban development plan by Jo Coenen, were to be situated on the south side of the KNSM Island (see 'Piraeus'). These superblocks are 170 metres long, 60 metres wide and eight storeys high. Albert's block is constructed in a neo-classical style and has a round plaza in its centre, with a large ornamental gate by Narcisse Tordoir in its southern entrance.

703 bus 42 ■

KNSM-laan, Levantkade
Hans Kollhoff & Christian Rapp
1994 Piraeus

Jo Coenen's urban development plan for the KNSM Island provided for a superblock on this site. In addition to a large number of standard rental flats, the building contains a number of special and more expensive apartments – a distinction that cannot be seen from the façade. Piraeus stands on the quay like a monumental sculpture. It embraces an historic KNSM building, creating an inner court in the middle of the building. The structure has been applauded for its careful detailing.

704 bus 42 ■

KNSM-laan
Wiel Arets
1995 Skydome

This sixty-metre high building lies in
the transitional zone between KNSM
Island and Java Island, and functions
as an important orientation point
in the Eastern Docklands. The slim
tower contains 100 owner-occupied
apartments divided over 22 storeys.
The façades are clad with dark grey
textured concrete plates, making it
appear that stone has been used.
Deep grooves in the tower suggest
that the building consists of pieces
shoved against one another. The
horizontal window strips temper
the vertical character of the tower.

705 bus 42 ■

Venetiëhof
Jo Coenen
1996 Emerald Empire

This circular building with a ring of
white single-family houses around it
is the final piece of the monumental
KNSM Island. The circular shape
assures optimal views of the IJ and
at the same time creates a sheltered
inner court. The building comprises
224 owner-occupied dwellings, the
vast majority of which are three-room
apartments. The alternation of balconies, loggias and voids creates
a varied and asymmetrical exterior.
A gateway leads to the public inner
court.

706 bus 42 ■

Sumatrakade and Javakade
Cruz & Ortiz
1996

Within the urban development plan for Java Island by Sjoerd Soeters, the Spanish architectural partnership Cruz & Ortiz designed six residential buildings for the quays. The basic design each time shows the same façade concept, with prefabricated façade elements of orange brick with joints of minimal width and sandwich panels with wooden sheets. The glass openings and loggias are cut into the surface of the façade as continuous horizontal strips. These buildings distinguish themselves from the others through a unity in the division of their façades and their restrained use of colour and materials.

707 bus 42 ■

C. van Eesterenlaan
A. van de Pol
1997 Rietlands Primary School

Ton van de Pol has placed a school on a triangular site next to the Piet Hein Tunnel and on the most important main artery of the Eastern Docklands. The school comprises sixteen classrooms, two playrooms and a sports facility. The façade, oriented to the adjoining playground, reflects the complexity of the building. The playground is situated on the sloping roof of the Piet Hein Tunnel.

708 tram 26 ■

Kees Brijdeplantsoen
DKV Architecten
1997

This project comprises three triangular sites at the intersection of the streets with the green strip which cuts across Sporenburg. The blocks contain single-family dwellings, maisonettes and office/home combinations. The latter are located in the points. Along the park the buildings are characterised by open, glazed façades that strengthen the relation between the public and private spheres. In contrast, the street façades are closed and flat, with perforations at various points.

709 tram 26 ■

J.F. van Hengelstraat, Ertskade
Neutelings Riedijk Architects
1997

In this project every dwelling has its own front door on the street, and a conservatory, roof terrace or garden. There are three types of residences, which all share the quality of having at least one storey that is of double width. The façade on the north side of the street is characterised by brick volumes that are interrupted on the second storey by recessed terraces. The south side of the street has been given protruding boxes of cedar wood which afford a view of the street.

710 bus 42 ■

Sumatrakade
Soeters Van Eldonk Architects
1999

The design of the façades of three of
the seven buildings on Java Island
by Sjoerd Soeters is derived from a
basic design, the most characteristic
element of which is the application
of strong colour fields in the façades.
Their easily recognised colours
cause these buildings to function as
landmarks. With their balconies and
extensions, the façades on the inner
areas, oriented to the south, are live-
lier than the closed façades on the
north sides.

711 bus 42 ■

Oostelijke Handelskade
Neutelings Riedijk Architects
1999 Residential tower

The tower marks the centre of the
Eastern Docklands area. The 20-storey
high tower contains apartments, with a
supermarket on the ground floor. The
plinth of the building is clad with dark
grey concrete, the tower with white
concrete plates. At various points the
façade is interrupted by holes in the
form of slits, squares or ells. These cavi-
ties assure that no two façades are the
same, and no two storeys have identical
ground plans. Aside from the holes,
it is the strips of windows, staggered in
relation to one another, which define
the façades.

712 tram 26 ■

Stuurmankade, P. Dijkstraplein
Dick van Gameren Architecten &
Bjarne Mastenbroek
(De Architectengroep) 1999

These residences at the tip of the Borneo peninsula are distinguished by the openness and their use of glass, concrete and wood in place of brick. In contrast to the much used internal parking place behind the façade, here an internal street has been created which runs the length of the block, off which the garages lie. Above the garages are patios, which provide sunlight for the northern oriented dwellings. The projecting, roofed terraces afford a vast panorama over the water.

713 tram 26 ■

Borneokade
Van Herk & De Kleijn
1999

The source of inspiration for the design was the elongated peninsulas and harbour mouths in the area. The wide façades were designed to convey the experience of extension. As a consequence, wedge-shaped dwellings were created that are alternately oriented to the north and south. The entrances are on the short side, while the living rooms are on the broad side with a beautiful view of the water. As well as maisonettes with street-level entrances, on the third layer the project includes small flats with conservatories on the south and dwellings with an elliptical living room on the fourth storey.

714 bus 43 ■

R.J.H. Fortuynplein
Koen van Velsen
1999 Pacman

The plan for the Borneo and
Sporenburg peninsulas included three
large residential blocks that would
break up the sea of patio residences.
These are very carefully positioned
on sight lines at prominent points in
the surroundings. Van Velsen's building is placed in line with the Oranje
Locks. In addition to luxury rental
apartments the building also includes
several stores and a parking garage.
The building is characterised by projecting balconies and a grid of wood
that hangs like a curtain in front of
the dark brown brick façade.

715 tram 26 ■

R.J.H. Fortuynplein
CASA
1999 De Oceaan

De Oceaan is the only former harbour
building that has been conserved on
Borneo. After rejecting the idea that
the building should become a part
of the adjoining Pacman building, CASA was asked to prepare a
design. The building was rebuilt into
studio dwellings and a restaurant.
The façades have been left intact as
much as possible.

716 tram 26 ■

Ertskade and Panamakade
Köther & Salman
1996-1999

The point of departure for the design for two locations on Sporenburg is the patio which is accessible through a gate on the street side. All spaces are grouped around this patio.

By keeping the walls as transparent as possible there are views through the house at countless points. The kitchen is found at the back on the first storey, with the living room on the street side. The bedroom and a roof terrace lie on the second storey. Except for the folding gates, the façades are characterised by the verticality of the small windows and French balconies.

717 tram 26 ■

Javakade
Karelse van der Meer
1998-1999

Karelse van der Meer realised seven buildings on Java Island, four on the Javakade and three on the Sumatra-kade. The four on the Sumatrakade look out over the IJ and the Jan Schaefer Bridge. The robust masonry façades with their small windows call up associations with warehouses. Dwellings alternate with commercial spaces on the ground floor. Prefabricated concrete screens behind which lie balconies characterise the buildings on the Java-kade. Each building has its own main colour: terracotta, anthracite and blue.

718 bus 42 ■

Seinwachterstraat and
D.L. Hudigstraat
M3H
1998-2000

In contrast to the patio dwelling generally used on Borneo-Sporenburg, M3H opted for a rhythm of built and vacant lots. With this design, the dwellings are not on the street or quay, but are oriented to the open spaces between them. All the dwellings are entered from grade level, some from the street and others from the interstices between them. The wooden planking on the garden façades is striking. These 'louvres' filter the entering light and increase privacy.

719 bus 43 ■

Brantasgracht, Lamonggracht and
Majanggracht
Art Zaaijer
1999

The architect has tried to realise a serenely designed house within the varied row of canal houses. The façade consists of a vertical strip of sun-repellant mirror glass, green glazed balustrades and aluminium sheets. On either side of this area stand brick piers that form a neutral link to the adjoining houses. The floor plan of the residence is determined by a stair in the corner on the garden side. This permits the plans for the different floors to remain open. A large roof terrace is a welcome addition to the modest back garden.

720 bus 42 ■

Brantasgracht and Lamonggracht
John Bosch
1999

A specific programme was developed for the canal house for double income couples without children. Each storey is high and as many views are created as possible. The internal division follows the classic arrangement of a canal house in which each storey has its own function. On the street side of the basement is an eat-in kitchen, with a second bathroom behind it. A stair connects the kitchen directly with the 'piano mobile' above it. Through the work-room the stair ends on the bedroom storey, that affords a view over the island.

721 bus 42 ∎

Borneokade
Josep Lluís Mateo
1999

The building lies at the head of Borneo Island and emphasises the extended form of the harbour pier through its horizontal articulation. The plinth contains a parking garage which receives daylight through its side façades. Because the dwellings are elevated with regard to the street, there is privacy, and views of the water are multiplied. The south side of the complex is clad with planking of tropical hardwood laid horizontally, the north side with brick. Occasionally the façade materials run in front of windows or terraces, helping to bind the complex together visually.

722 bus 43 ∎

Scheepstimmermanstraat 42
Rowin Petersma
1999 Private residence

The façades of this modern canal house are to a great extent composed of Corten steel, material that refers to the area's former character as a harbour. Like most houses in the Scheepstimmermanstraat, this house is oriented to the back because of the water and the southern exposure. For that reason the southern façade contains considerable glass, while that on the street side is more closed, for the sake of privacy. Here, alongside the entry, is a 4.5 metre high carport. Thanks to a mechanical system, two autos can be parked there, one above the other.

723 bus 43 ■

Scheepstimmermanstraat 62
Rapp & Rapp
1999 Private residence

The peculiarity of this dwelling is that it is twice cut through lengthwise with a long slit. On the ground floor this creates an internal street, with entrances to the dwelling half way back on both sides. The street ends with a stair to the water. The second slit, on the top storey, functions as an extended terrace that can be incorporated into the dwelling by opening sliding doors. The design and use of materials in the façades expresses the stately character of an Amsterdam canal house.

724 bus 43 ■

Scheepstimmermanstraat 116
FARO Architecten
1999 Private residence

This structure contains two elements. The backbone of the design consists of a stair which runs like a waterfall through the whole house along the right side of the floor plan. On the first storey the living space has a balcony on the south side, and on top of the house there is a roof terrace. On the street side there is an introverted façade with a perforated concrete screen. During the day the openings in the wall filter the daylight that enters.

725 bus 43 ■

Scheepstimmermanstraat 120
Koen van Velsen
1999 Private residence

This house is part of a wall of private homes designed by various architects. The front and back façades each consist of a heavy, black concrete screen, which together form the shell of the house. The screens are pierced by large horizontal light openings. The bottom portion of the concrete screen on the front can be folded up, allowing access to the dwelling. Here one finds the parking place and a patio with a tree that grows up through the roof.

726 bus 43 ■

Stuurmankade, Scheepstimmermanstraat
Enric Miralles
1999

This project by the Spanish architect Miralles is a striking presence in the midst of the houses in the area, chiefly clad with red brick. On each side of a passageway Miralles designed six dwellings. The houses have an elongated, geniculate ground plan that runs from front to back through the whole lot. Four of the dwellings have ground level entrances, the other two are stacked. The façades of the dwellings are clad with strikingly coloured glazed brick.

727 bus 43 ■

P.E. Tegelbergplein, Seinwachterstraat
Claus en Kaan
2000 Panorama dwellings

As was prescribed for all the dwellings in the Borneo-Sporenburg planning area, the panorama dwellings have an internal parking place and a ground floor height of 3.5 metres. Most of the dwellings have a living room on the first storey and an internal terrace on the second. Lining the façade inside the light well with glass permits the back section of the house to also receive considerable daylight. The frontages overlooking the water are distinguished by floor-to-ceiling glass façades.

728 bus 42 ■

Brantasgracht and Lamonggracht
Dana Ponec (Soeters Van Eldonk
Ponec Architecten)
2000

Dana Ponec took inspiration from
the classic canal houses with a great
entrance hall as the division between
the street and the private domain. The
house therefore has been given a stair
and raised stoop on the street side
with behind it a kitchen/family-room
on the garden side. Above this lies the
living room with a large, square bay
window on the street side. On the garden side a void creates a spatial connection with the kitchen. A stair leads
to the bedrooms and a roof terrace.

729 bus 42 ■

Scheepstimmermanstraat 26
MVRDV
2000 Private residence

By building on only half of the relatively
deep lot, an 'alley' is created along
with the very narrow house, only 2.5
metres wide. There is a glass façade
running the full height and length of
the house along the areaway. This ori-
entates the house to the areaway and
creates a very wide house in place of
the small house. In the alley is a storage area with a sloping roof on which
an auto can be parked, and two pro-
trusions bulge from the glass façade,
arching over the areaway. The alley is
lighted, so that it also continues its
relation to the interior into the evening.

730 bus 43 ■

Baron G.A. Tindalplein
De Architekten Cie.
(Frits van Dongen)
2001 The Whale

The Whale is one of the three planned 'superblocks'. At the head and tail the silver-coloured building is tipped up, creating views through to the water, and public and private space gradually shade into one another. The oblique roof lines are derived from studies regarding the angle of the sun, and facilitate optimal penetration by sunlight. The crushed shape of the building creates unusual dwellings on the top and bottom storeys. The garden in the centre is designed by West 8.

731 bus 42 ■

Java Island/Oostelijke Handelskade
Venhoeven CS
2001 Jan Schaefer Bridge

The head of Java Island is connected to the Oostelijke Handelskade by the 280 metre long Jan Schaefer Bridge, running right through the Willem de Zwijger warehouse, 1933/34, a structure retained from the old harbour, which was renovated by André van Stigt in 2007. Passing through this building creates an abrupt change of scenery. In his design Venhoeven emphasised the various currents of traffic on the bridge by means of differences in height and width. Considerable attention is devoted to the lighting, which contributes to the unusual experience that crossing the bridge should be.

732 tram 26 ■

Maria Austriastraat
Zeinstra Van der Pol
(Herman Zeinstra)
2001 KPN telephone exchange

In order to provide each home with a telephone connection in a timely manner, this
telephone exchange was the first building on IJburg. The structure is a closed
box in which countless cables surface.
It is unmanned; people are present only
now and then, for maintenance. Climate
control and security concerns demanded
a closed skin. The façades are made of
semi-transparent glass panels with narrow, horizontal coloured plastic plates.
It is to these that the building owes its
mystical aura.

733 tram 26

De Rietlanden
Venhoeven CS &
Hans van Heeswijk
2001 Park Towers

Ten silver-coloured towers are placed
in a park in the centre of the Eastern
Docklands. The western-most five towers in each case consist of two structural elements what are displaced in
respect to one another and separated
from each other by a glass stairwell.
The eastern-most four towers contain
owner-occupied dwellings. A fifth, brick
tower contains government subsidised
rental units. Particularly in the towers with sales units, the maximum of
vari-ation has been achieved. No two
storeys are the same in the 'robot-like'
towers.

734 tram 26

De Rietlanden
Rudy Uytenhaak Architectenbureau
2002 'Hoop, Liefde en Fortuin'

The differentiated programme led to the
realisation of a multi-faceted complex of
buildings for various lifestyles. The complex is comprised of areas which cross
and overlap one another and are clad
with different materials. This complexity is
a means of introducing scale and rhythm
at all levels, and making connections.
The sloping north façade consists of a
concrete screen in which the windows are
recessed. The front functions as a 'veil';
only when one comes closer to the black
dots on the concrete and the dwellings
which lie behind it become visible.

735 tram 26 ■

Azartplein
Diener & Diener
2002 Hoogkade, Laagkade

At the head of the causeway, at the
point where Java and KNSM Islands
come together, lies the third 'superblock' from Jo Coenen's plan for KNSM
Island. Consisting of two separate
residential buildings on opposite sides
of the Verbindingsdam, this complex
functions not only as a gateway to this
residential neighbourhood, but also as
a link between the two urban planning
visions for the Islands. The monotony
and flatness of the façades is striking,
and permits the complex to be a point
of rest visually in this garishly coloured
area.

736 tram 10 ■

IJburglaan
Maccreanor Lavington Architects
2003

This complex is one of the first buildings
on IJburg, and includes dwellings with
very large dimensions. The goal was to
produce a multifunctional building that
affords flexibility for changes in function
over time. Among the ways this has been
accomplished is extra height on each
storey. The roominess of the dwellings is
emphasised by large windows, voids and
extra light penetration from above. The
dwellings each have their own entrance
from ground level.
The robust dark brown brick façades are
interrupted by large balconies on the
water side.

737 tram 26 ■

Oostelijke Handelskade 34
E. Breman, 1918
MVRDV (interior, 2004)
2004 Lloyd Hotel

At the beginning of the 20th century the
Lloyd Hotel served as temporary accom-
modations for the emigrants who came
from Eastern Europe before leaving for
South and Central America on ships of
the Royal Dutch Lloyd Line. After standing empty for years, the façades, leaded
glass windows and canopy construction are restored and the building is
renovated as a hotel for artists and art
lovers. MVRDV produced a design for the
interior which combines the old character
of the building with new elements. There
are 120 rooms, a library and a cultural
embassy.

738 tram 10, 26 ■

Piet Heinkade 3
Nielsen, Nielsen & Nielsen
2005 Muziekgebouw/
BIMhuis

A centre for modern music has risen
at the head of an extended quay. The
architects have designed a building that
accommodate concert halls, studios,
practice rooms, documentation centres
and restaurants and cafes. The building
includes a high glass hall into which
the concert halls of the former IJsbreker
and BIMhuis music centres have been
inserted. The outside walls have beern
executed entirely in double glass so that
vis-itors are surrounded by a magnificent view of the IJ.

739 tram 16 ■

Oostelijke Handelskade
Köther & Salman, Wingender
Hovenier, Herder & Van der Neut
2006 De Loodsen

A mix of old warehouses and new buildings has arisen along the most important artery between the renewed Eastern
Docklands and the city centre. The strip
is divided up into elongated blocks that
were filled in by various architects. The
complex includes 300 dwellings, offices
and commercial spaces, a portion of
which were delivered as shells, to stimu-
late having a small business run from
home. Interior courts, each with a different design, will enliven the complex.

740 tram 26 ■

Zuidbuurt
Marc Koehler Architect
2007 Huis IJburg

This cubiform dwelling is eye-catching for its black façade, in which the bricks project noticeably now and then. Within several years however a large part of this façade will be overgrown by various climbing plants, roses, kiwi fruit and grapevines. The greenery will later afford the residents protection and privacy. Ultimately birds and insects will also make use of the green coat, so that the house becomes a part of an urban eco-system in a creative and enduring way.

741 tram 26 ■

Steiger Island
Architectenbureau Marlies Rohmer
2009 Water residences, IJburg

On the north side of the enclosed water feature on Steiger Island 55 dwellings have been realised in an urban water-side neighbourhood. The dwellings vary from expensive owner-occupied residences to subsidised rentals. The variation in spacing and placement achieves a loose, informal parcellation, so that despite the approach as a single project the adventure of living on the water is preserved. The floating dwellings lie in concrete tanks which are tied up to piles, and connected to jetties by shoring.

742 tram 26 ■

Latest projects (2005-2010)

In the second half of this decade the scene in Amsterdam was dominated by large-scale urban renewal operations in post-war neighbourhoods. The renewal of the Bijlmermeer, begun in the early 1990s, approached its completion. A large number of the characteristic honeycomb flat buildings surrounded by greenery were replaced by low-rise housing. The smaller-scale new construction is made up primarily of owner-occupied dwellings, in an effort to achieve greater social diversification and a more pleasant living environment. In terms of the urban development plan, in addition to the demolition of the existing buildings that meant eliminating the embankments on which motorised traffic had run, so that automotive, bicycle and foot traffic were no longer strictly separated from one another. The post-war shibboleth about the separation of functions was also thrown overboard; in the new urban development plan homes, shopping and workplaces were combined to the maximum extent possible. The Anton de Komplein near the ArenA and the Amsterdamse Poort shopping mall became the new heart of the district, with spectacular access from the redeveloped Amsterdam Bijlmer station.

For several years now Nieuw West in Amsterdam has also been undergoing a fundamental redevelopment. The functionalist strip parcellation of the 1950s and 1960s, a heritage of the pre-war General Expansion Plan (AUP), has made way for a freer composition of buildings, in which the choice has often been made for closed blocks of buildings with striking architectonic design. In this section of the city too the effort is being made to achieve a less uniform population composition. Light, space and green – Van Eesteren's design principles – have yielded to higher building density and more architectonic variation. Although many of the post-war buildings are of abominable quality, a handful of criticasters have raised questions about the fundamental settling up with the original organisation of the neighbourhoods of Geuzenveld-Slotermeer, Slotervaart, Osdorp and Bos en Lommer. Despite its critics, the architecture in the renewal projects in the Bijlmermeer and Nieuw West has received praise both in The Netherlands and internationally – the reason why this chapter includes a large number of these new projects.

The city centre was also subject to many infrastructural interventions in this period. In addition to re-profiling and the redirection of traffic flow, it is particularly the construction of the North/South metro line that has been exercising minds. In the summer of 2008 a number of designated architectural monuments beside the excavations on the Vijzelgracht began subsiding; as a result, the city decided to all but halt work on the metro line in the city centre. Work resumed in the summer of 2009, but the construction delays mean that the metro will not be in service until 2017 at the earliest.

The financial crisis that burst with such fury in the summer of 2008 particularly left its traces in the building world. Architects lost their jobs, work was suspended and future projects were blown away. Precisely at this same time many of the office complexes in the Zuidas came on the market; because of the crisis, to this day they have only sporadically attracted tenants. In view of the architectonic quality and central location of the Zuidas, it is doubtful if that will remain the case much longer. There are more serious problems with the out-of-the-way and monotonous office parks in Sloterdijk and Bullewijk, locations where it is a question whether they will ever be successful, at least in their present form.

The Zuidas is not the only place in Amsterdam where lots of construction is going on; in Amsterdam North there is also a whole new part of the city in the works. With the modern EYE Film Institute as its cultural centrepiece, Overhoeks will soon be a new office and residential neighbourhood with views over the IJ. The development of the district comes in conjunction with the emergence of the NDSM shipyard as a haven for creative industry, which has been confirmed in adventurous architectonic designs such as the Kraanspoor. Both the north and south banks of the IJ – the latter primarily thanks to the new construction on the Oosterdok and Westerdok – are increasingly being integrated with the city centre. A neighbourhood with 5500 dwellings will arise at the mouth of the IJ, on Zeeburger Island, and the recently delivered water dwellings near IJburg appear to have sparked off a national trend for building on the water. All these developments guarantee a unique and thrilling future for Amsterdam architecture.

The Nescio Bridge over the Amsterdam - Rhine Canal

Spaklerweg
Architectuurstudio Herman Hertzberger
2005 Headquarters AGV/DWR

This double office tower stands in a bend
of the Amstel River, precisely at the point
where the river flows across the city
limits. In designing the two towers the
choice was made for sea-green glass,
which draws striking contours through
the aluminium-coloured façade. The four
bridges between the towers are incorporated into the whole pattern of this glass.
The section of the city where the towers
are located – between the Amstel, railway
and A10 motorway – is presently being
developed as the 'Amstel Quarter', an
integrated living and working area.

801 metro 51, 53, 54 ■

De Boelelaan
Jeanne Dekkers architecture
2006 Opleidingsinstituut Zorg en
Welzijn

Over the past decade the Vrije Universiteit
has enormously expanded its campus on
the De Boelelaan. One of the architectonic highlights on the site is the OZW
building, suddenly rising up from the
lawns like a softly slanted sculpture. The
red brick, the projecting window frames
and the friendly form of the building is
reminiscent of work of the Amsterdam
School. Educational institutions for health
care and social welfare workers are
brought together within its walls. In the
heart of the building a cascade of voids
with escalators and bridges connects the
various collective spaces.

802 tram 5, metro 51 □

Evertsweertplantsoen
Dok Architects
2006 Brede School Osdorp

What are called 'broad schools' are a new trend in school architecture. The idea is that different educational and social service institutions are brought together in one building, to encourage interaction among their various clients and users. There are two elementary schools, a day-care centre and a municipal health authority facility housed in the Brede School Osdorp. The design is conspicuous for the bright green façades, which have earned it the nickname 'The Frog'.

803 tram 17 ☐

Jan van Galenstraat
Soeters Van Eldonk
2006 Pyramids

At 55 metres in height, these two almost identical pyramids of dwellings are a spectacular addition to Amsterdam's skyline. The use of brick and the stepped, receding façades give the buildings a friendly, playful aura. That contrasts with the brusque and boring commercial structure of the adjoining Food Center, separated from the pyramids by the busy Jan van Galenstraat and a wide entrance plaza. The buildings merely suggest an enlargement of traditional Dutch step gables.

804 tram 3 ■

Jan van Galenstraat
VenhoevenCS Architects
2006 SportPlaza Mercator

This sports centre merges perfectly
into its green surroundings in the
Rembrandtpark. The capricious forms
of the building, in combination with the
green-clad façades, give it the appearance of a weed-covered hill rising out
of the park. The walls of the sports
centre have 50,000 plants growing in
them, which are supplied with water and
nutrients through an ingenious drainage
system. Among the facilities accommodated by the complex are various kinds
of swimming pools, a bathhouse and a
fitness centre.

805 tram 7 □

Dr. H. Colijnstraat
MVRDV
2007 Residential building,
Eendrachtspark

Since the renewal of the Western Garden
Cities began, architecture lovers have
been coming to this part of the city in
increasing numbers, thanks in part to the
unusual design of this apartment complex
in Geuzenveld. The enormous gaps in the
façade play host to open, shared spaces,
where a number of oversized flowerpots
stand. The whole is picked out in light by
likewise oversized chandeliers. Daylight
floods everywhere into the block through the
openings, and the residents have a view of
the Eendrachtspark. With its unique architecture this project counts as a pioneering
design in the restructuring of Nieuw West.

806 tram 13 □

Strawinskylaan
David Chipperfield Architects
2007 Freshfields Bruckhaus Deringer

Until several years ago this building
housed the Insurance Exchange, but then
stood entirely empty until its total renovation. The original design was from 1988.
Despite its short life span the style and
quality rapidly became outdated, so that
the building no longer fit in with the brand
new glass and steel Zuidas. On the exterior the façade on the entrance side was
entirely stripped and clad with anthracite,
and provided with new window frames
and glass. The adaptations have led to a
more transparent and friendly building, in
which a law firm is now located.

807 tram 5, metro 50, 51 ■

Hoekenrode
N. Grimshaw
2007 Station, Amsterdam Bijlmer Arena

With the transformation of the area
around the Arena into a high-quality office
location and venue for events, and the
completion of the direct rail link between
Utrecht and Schiphol, the expansion
and improvement of the train and metro
station became an urgent priority. The
new design allows more daylight in and
integrates the new Arena Boulevard with
the Amsterdamse Poort shopping centre.
The expanded station has an organically
shaped roof of glass and steel, clad on
the inside with wooden panels. The length
of the platforms, which are almost entirely
covered and further increase the volume
of the structure, is also striking.

808 metro 50, 54 □

Kraanspoor / Ms Oslofjordweg
Trude Hooykaas Design Group
2007 Kraanspoor

The concrete structure lying parallel to the quay is a former craneway, along which supertankers were moored in the past to be broken up. The 270-meter-long structure was designed in 1952 by the architect J.D. Postma. During a 1997 bicycle tour of the NDSM wharf Trude Hooykaas had the idea of placing an office building on the craneway. The idea resulted in a three storey building entirely encased in glass, which when viewed from the city on the other side of the IJ appears to hover above the water.

809 NDSM ferry ■

Oosterdokskade
Jo Coenen & Co
2007 Public Library

The new central library has hardly anything in common with the classic lending library with reading rooms. Coenen's building is a multifunctional complex where, in addition to borrowing books, one can also study, listen to audio material, and get a bite to eat. This multifunctionality is reflected in the eclectic design, with its entrance recessed in the natural stone front façade. This creates a spacious entry plaza with an overhanging canopy. In the interior he opted for white as the dominant colour, a choice which was prompted primarily by the limited incidence of light within the building.

810 tram 4, 9, 16, 24, 25, 26, metro 51, 53, 54 □

Oeverpad
DKV Architecten
2007 Schutterstoren

This residential tower on the Sloterplas is part of the urban renewal operation Meer en Oever, in which the original urban development plan with its parallel residential blocks is being partially replaced by a freer composition of buildings. The residential tower on the water is to be an accent for the neighbourhood – the reason why the architect opted for an eye-catching cylindrical shape, resting on a narrow base. The accent is enhanced even more by the small earthen mound on which the tower was built, concealing within it parking places for the residents.

811 tram 17 ■

Oosterdokskade
de Architekten Cie.
2008 Conservatorium

The location of this glass building by Frits van Dongen on Oosterdokseiland brings with it easy accessibility and beautiful views, but is also accompanied by the requisite noise from passing trains. This led to the choice of a construction in which the glass façade envelopes the actual building. The division of the storeys is strongly functional; the public part takes up the bottom five floors; classrooms and practice spaces are found in the middle section, and the top floor provides space for an entresol and bar with a view out over the city.

812 tram 4, 9, 16, 24, 25, 26, metro 51, 53, 54 □

Van Heenvlietlaan
Claus and Kaan Architects
2008 District Council Public Works
Depot, Zuideramstel

Buitenveldert is a chic neighbourhood,
and anyone looking at this depot from
outside could be forgiven for thinking it is
an urban villa rather than centre for park
maintenance, neighbourhood services,
civil engineering and street cleaning. The
sterile white walls conceal workshops
and storage areas, as well as dozens of
maintenance trucks and street sweepers.
The walls are broken by several wooden
entrance gates and strikingly low windows, by turns recessed and placed flat
in the façade.

813 tram 5, metro 51 ■

Carolina MacGillavrylaan
HVDN Architects
2008 Het Kasteel

Over the past few years the Science Park
in Watergraafsmeer has been transformed
into a full-fledged section of the city,
with its own train station and a myriad
of scientific and university institutes. In
2008 the first dwellings in the area were
delivered, one of which, Het Kasteel, can
be accounted the most striking presence
in the street scene. The name of this residential complex refers to the U-shaped
low-rise building and an inner court that
can be accessed by means of a bridge
over a 'moat'. The glass façade that surrounds the building is intended to protect
it from the noise nuisance from the
nearby railway marshalling yard.

814 tram 9 □

Anton de Komplein
Vera Yanovshtchinsky architects
2008 Bijlmer Sport Centrum

The Anton de Komplein is destined to become a lively urban plaza. For this reason a transparent design was chosen for the sports centre, so that those working out inside can see the passers-by outside – and vice versa. The transparency is intensified by the use of a lot of glass and a refreshing shade of green, which optically links the different functions in the building.

815 metro 50, 54 ☐

Anton de Komplein
Architectenbureau Paul de Ruiter
2009 Bijlmer Parktheater

The renewal of Amsterdam Zuidoost has been under way for two decades now and is approaching its completion. The Bijlmer Parktheater is one of the cultural keystones. The building, with its flexible programming, is situated on the edge of a large city park and the Anton de Komplein, which in the future will be the beating heart of the Bijlmermeer. During the day, with its oval design and a façade of glass, corrugated steel sheets and wooden strips, it is a striking presence, but when darkness falls the atmosphere becomes yet more extravagant thanks to scores of LED lamps.

816 metro 50, 54 ☐

Leidseplein
Jonkman Klinkhamer, architecture interiors urban planning
2009 Rabo Auditorium

The lack of an auditorium with a flat floor led the Stadsschouwburg and the Toneelgroep Amsterdam to an innovative idea; in cooperation with the Melkweg they chose to build a new auditorium *across* the property lines of the cultural venues. The massive new block of steel and aluminium – actually a building on a building – is broken by a projecting glass window and an entirely open rehearsal space on the ground floor. The new auditorium has a capacity of over 500 seats.

817 tram 1, 2, 5, 7, 10 ☐

Europaplein
Benthem Crouwel Architects
2009 RAI Elicium

In this design one is immediately struck by the 'folded' lines of the façade, which swing through the building as a powerful S-shape and separate the glass front façade from the stainless steel back façade. The Elicium houses convention and presentation facilities, as well as offices and a multi-purpose ballroom. The building is comprised of a horizontal section on which a 47- meter-high tower has been placed. The realisation of this expansion confirms the intentions of the City and the RAI to remain in the present location until 2024 in any case – an intention prompted by the development of the Zuidas.

818 tram 4 ■

Claude Debussylaan
(designed by) Erick van Egeraat
2009 Erick van Egeraat tower

Like the other buildings the Mahler4-block this office tower carries the name of the architect, but at first the structure bore the working title 'The Rock'. The name refers to the upper storeys, which are wrapped with a combination of polyester and natural stone so that this section has the appearance of having been hewn out of rock. The exuberant architecture arises from the urban development assignment for the Zuidas: all the buildings must have a plinth, central zone and top. The architect has made this condition explicitly visible in his design.

819 tram 5, metro 50, 51 ■

Funenpark
NL Architects
2009 Verdana

With its whimsical form this building could be regarded as a BLOB. But what is perhaps the most striking element in the design, the roof, is not visible from the street side. The sloping roof, set with moss and grass, creates the impression of a hill landscape that is perforated by openings in which the roof terraces of the dwellings are found. One of the façades of the building, cut through by an interior street, is rendered with gold-coloured window frames. With all these peculiar elements Verdana stands out among the other straightforward blocks in the Funenpark.

820 tram 10 ■

Funenpark
Dick van Gameren architects
2009 Blok J

The Funen is a former industrial site and rail yard adjoining the eastern city centre. Like the Oostelijk Havengebied, lying on the other side of the railway line, the Funen has been developed into a residential area with high quality architecture. Block J is a very compact and urban residential block, where a relatively large number of people live in a limited number of square meters – a degree of density previously achieved in the Westerdok. The most striking element in the design is the set of six free-standing one family dwellings on the roof.

821 tram 10 ■

Amstel
Hans van Heeswijk architects
2009 Hermitage Amsterdam

In 2004 the Hermitage moved into the Amstelhof, a former nursing home that had served that function for over 300 years. It was only in 2007 however that a start was made on its definitive transformation into an exhibition space. The renovation of the square building took place in phases, one wing at a time, restoring as much of the old splendour as possible. For instance, a large number of the intermediate floors constructed in the 1970s had to be demolished. With the renovation a closed and introverted building began a new life as an inviting public domain devoted to art and culture.

822 tram 9, 14, metro 51, 53, 54 □

Meerpad
Heren 5 Architects
2009 Meerpad

New construction projects utilising historicising architecture have been delivered for occupancy with increasing frequency in recent years. The Meerpad, lying in rustic surroundings just behind the Nieuwendammerdijk, is one of the latest examples of this trend. The Dutch provinciality is expressed in the use of a hipped roof and red brick in all 70 homes, which together form a secluded neighbourhood. The separate parcels are uniformly arranged, but as one approaches the water the dwellings become increasingly narrower and higher. Historicising architecture is very much in demand by the general public. These dwellings were sold out in no time at all.

823 bus 32 ■

Boomgaardlaan
Rudy Uytenhaak Architectenbureau
(urban development plan)
2009 De Bongerd

Amsterdam North is known for its garden towns from the beginning of the 20th century. This urban development plan wanted to link up with that tradition of rustic building, and provides for the construction of 1600 dwellings on a former allotment garden complex and industrial site. Despite the choice for separate parcels with ample gardens, high density is achieved by keeping the streets narrow. The free-standing residences are divided into seven typologies; each type was designed by a renowned architect in both modern and more traditional styles.

824 bus 38 from Buiksloterwegveer ■

Jan van Zutphenplantsoen
Wiel Arets
2009 Four towers

These four apartment blocks of eleven
stories each are characterised by hyper-
modern design that reaches back to the
principles of the AUP; light, air and space
in spaciously conceived strip construction.
The flat buildings stand with their head
end on a large lake, which offers views
over park-like environs. The bands on the
façades, separating large quantities of
glass, are of white aluminium, giving the
architecture a particular clarity and transparency. The towers, lying on the rural
edge of Osdorp, accommodate a total of
390 apartments.

825 tram 1 ■

Gustav Mahlerlaan
UNStudio
2010 UNStudio tower

Like many buildings in the Zuidas, these
towers proceed from the idea of flexible
office arrangement, with large voids and
grand views. The voids assure abundant
penetration by daylight, which likewise
enters through the horizontal white façade
elements that vary in thickness depend-
ing on their orientation to the sun. The
85-meter-high tower is the keystone in
the development of the sub-area Mahler4,
where in recent years many dwellings and
stores have been realised in addition to
office space.

826 tram 5, metro 50, 51 ■

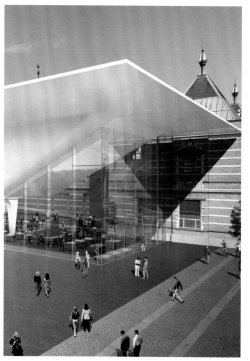

Museumplein
Benthem Crouwel
2011 Expansion Stedelijk Museum

Like many other museums around the
Museumplein, the Stedelijk is being renovated and enlarged. And like many other
museums the work has fallen behind
schedule; the expectation is now that the
Stedelijk can again open its doors early
in 2011. Then visitors will no longer enter
this temple of modern art from the Paulus
Potterstraat, but via a new main entrance
on the Museumplein. The expansion on the
Museumplein side – on the site of the former
Sandberg wing – has a light and transparent
character, with lots of glass and a large canopy of plastic. For its shape, the extension
has already been nicknamed 'the bathtub'.

827 tram 2, 3, 5, 12, 16 ☐

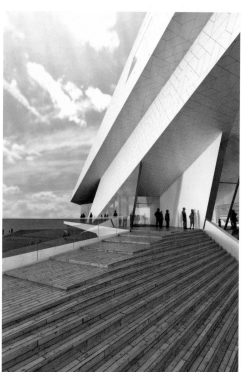

Overhoeks
Delugan Meissl Associated Architects
2011 EYE Film Institute

The redevelopment of the northern banks
of the IJ has picked up speed with the construction of the new urban neighbourhood
of Overhoeks, and with its opening at the
end of 2011 the EYE Film Institute will be
an eccentric attention-getter there. That is
primarily the result of the building's location
on a spit of land (in part the result of land-
fill) in the IJ, but the white sculptural form of
the museum will also draw the eye. The film
museum will soon accommodate four film
auditoriums, an information centre, library
and exhibition spaces.

828 Buiksloterweg ferry ☐

Further reading

Abrahamse, J.E., *De grote uitleg van Amsterdam. Stadsontwikkeling in de zeventiende eeuw*, Bussum, 2010

d'Ailly. A.E., *Historische Gids van Amsterdam*, Amsterdam, 1949

ARCAM, *Architectuurkaart Amsterdam*, Amsterdam, 2009

Baar, P.-P. de, et al., *The Amstel*, Amsterdam, 2002

Baart, J.M., *Het 'Kasteel van Amstel' burch of bruggehoofd*, Amsterdam, 1995

Bakker, B. *Amsterdam and his ring of canals*, Bussum, 2009

Bakker, M.M. & F.M. van de Poll, *Architectuur en Stedebouw in Amsterdam 1850-1940*, Zwolle, 1992

Barbieri, S.U. & L. van Duin, *Honderd jaar Nederlandse Architectuur 1901-2000. Tendenzen en hoogtepunten*, Nijmegen, 1999

Beek, M., *Drie eeuwen Amsterdamse Bouwkunst, architectuurtekeningen*, Amsterdam, 1984

Beekum, R. van, *B.T. Boeyinga, Amsterdamse School architect*, Bussum, 2003

Behm, M. & M. Kloos, (preface Cees Nooteboom) *25 buildings you should have seen*, Amsterdam, 2008

Bock, M., *Anfänge einer neuen Architektur. Berlages Beitrag zur architektonischen Kultur der Niederlande im ausgehende 19. Jahrhundert*, 's-Gravenhage/Wiesbaden, 1983

Bock, M., et al., *Berlage in Amsterdam*, Amsterdam, 1992

Bock, M., *Michel de Klerk. Architect and artist of the Amsterdam School*, Rotterdam 1997

Boer, N. de, *Strategische plekken in Amsterdam*, Amsterdam, 1994

Boeken, A., *Amsterdamse Stoepen*, Amsterdam, 1950

Boterenbrood, H. & J. Prang, *Van der Mey en het Scheepvaarthuis*, 's-Gravenhage, 1989

Bruijne, D., et al., *Amsterdam Zuidoost – Southeast*, Bussum 2002

Buch, J., *A Century of Dutch Architecture in the Netherlands 1880-1980*, Rotterdam, 1993

Buurman, M. & M. Kloos, *Amsterdam Architecture 1997-99*, Amsterdam, 2000

Buurman, M. & M. Kloos, *Amsterdamse Architectuur 2000-2002 / Amsterdam Architecture 2000-2002*, Amsterdam, 2003

Buurman, M. & M. Kloos, *IMPACT, Amsterdamse stedebouw na 1986*, Amsterdam, 2005

Casciato, M., *Amsterdam School*, Rotterdam, 1996

Colenbrander, B., Style: *Standard and Signature in Dutch Architecture*, Rotterdam, 1993

Deben, L. & W. Salet, *Cultural heritage and the future of the historic inner city of Amsterdam*, Amsterdam, 2004

Dien, A. van, et al., *Nederlandse Architectuur en Stedebouw 1945-1980*, Amsterdam, 1984

Dijkshoorn, W. (ed.), *Amsterdamse Grachtentuinen Herengracht*, Zwolle, 1998

Elfrink, R. (ed.), *Berlage en de Toekomst van Amsterdam Zuid*, Rotterdam, 1992

Fanelli, G., *Moderne Architectuur in Nederland 1900-1940*, 's-Gravenhage, 1975

Fraenkel, F.F., *Het plan Amsterdam-Zuid van Berlage*, Alphen aan den Rijn, 1976

Frank, S.S., *Michel de Klerk 1884-1923*, Ann Arbor, 1984

Fremantle, K., *The Baroque Town Hall of Amsterdam*, Utrecht, 1959

Gaillard, K. (ed.), *Berlage en Amsterdam Zuid*, Rotterdam, 1992

Groenendijk, P. & P. Vollaard, *Guide to Modern Architecture in Amsterdam*, Rotterdam, 1996

Haagsma, I., et al., *Amsterdamse Gebouwen 1880-1980*, Utrecht 1981

Haan, H. de, et al., *Terug naar de straat. De vernieuwing van de F-buurt*, Amsterdam Zuidoost, Haarlem, 2004

Haaren, M. van, et al., *Atlas 19de eeuwse Ring Amsterdam*, Amsterdam 2004

Hameleers, H., *Kaarten van Amsterdam 1866/2000*, Bussum, 2002

Heinemeijer, W.F. et al., *Amsterdam in Kaarten*, Ede, 1987

Hellinga, H. et al., *Algemeen Uitbreidingsplan 50 jaar*, Amsterdam, 1985

Hitchcock, H.R., *Netherlandish Scrolled Gables of the Sixteenth and Seventeenth Centuries*, New York, 1978

Hoeven, C. van der & J. Louwe, *Amsterdam als Stedelijk Bouwwerk*, Amsterdam, 2003

Hoog, M. de, *4x Amsterdam. Ontwerpen aan de stad*, Bussum, 2005

Hoog, M. de, R. Vermeulen, *New Rhythms of the city. Moulding the metropolis in Amsterdam*, Bussum, 2009

Hoogewoud, G., et al., *P.J.H. Cuypers en Amsterdam*, 's-Gravenhage, 1985

Hooykaas, T., *Kraanspoor*, Amsterdam, 2009

Huisken, J. (ed.) et al., *Jacob van Campen: het klassieke ideaal in de Gouden Eeuw*, Amsterdam, 1995

Huisman, J., et al., *100 jaar bouwkunst in Amsterdam/An outline of Amsterdam Architecture since 1900*, Amsterdam, 1999

Idsinga, T. & J. Schilt, *W. van Tijen (1894-1974)*, 's-Gravenhage, 1985

Janse, H., *Building Amsterdam*, Amsterdam, 1993

Janse, H., *De Oude Kerk te Amsterdam. Bouwgeschiedenis en restauratie*, Zwolle, 2004

Jolles, A. (ed.), *Planning Amsterdam. Scenarios for urban development 1928-2003*, Rotterdam, 2003

Jolles, A., et al., *Eastern Harbour District Amsterdam. Urbanism and Architecture*, Rotterdam, 2006

Kessel, E. van & M. Kuperus, *M. Staal-Kropholler (1891-1966)*, Rotterdam, 1991

Killiam, T. & H. Tulleners, *Amsterdam Canal Guide*, Utrecht, 1978

Kleijn, K., et al., *Nederlandse Bouwkunst, een geschiedenis van tien eeuwen architectuur*, Alphen aan den Rijn, 1995

Kloos, M. (ed.), *Amsterdam, an architectural lesson*, Amsterdam, 1988

Kloos, M. (ed.), *Public Interiors: architecture and public life inside Amsterdam*, Amsterdam, 1993

Kloos, M. (ed.), *Amsterdam Architecture 1991-1993*, Amsterdam, 1994

Kloos, M. (ed.), *Amsterdam's High-Rise*, Amsterdam, 1995

Kloos, M. (ed.), *Amsterdam Architecture 1994-97 (ARCAM Pocket 11)*, Amsterdam, 1997

Kloos, M. & D. Wendt, *Formats for Living*, Amsterdam, 2000

Kloos, M. (ed.), *Ring A10/Ringroad Amsterdam*, Amsterdam, 2010

Kohlenbach, B., *P.L Kramer, architect van de*

Amsterdamse School, Naarden, 1994

Kok, A.A., *Amsterdamse Woonhuizen*, Amsterdam, 1941

Koopmans, Y., *Muurvast en gebeiteld / Fixed and chiselled, sculpture in architecture 1840-1940*, Rotterdam, 1994

Koster, E., *Eastern Docklands Amsterdam*, Amsterdam, 1995

Kuipers, M.C., et al., *Jongere Bouwkunst, Amsterdam binnen de Singelgracht (1850-1940)*, Zeist, 1984

Kuypers, W., *Dutch Classicist Architecture*, Delft, 1980

Kuypers, W., *Triumphant Entry of Renaissance Architecture into the Netherlands*, Alphen aan den Rijn, 1994

Laar, F. van, *Amsterdam woont hier... volkshuisvesting en stadsvernieuwing tussen tussen 1972 en 1994*, Amsterdam, 1994

Lansink, L., *De Geschiedenis van het Amsterdamse Stationsplein*, Amsterdam, 1982

Leonhardt, G., *Amsterdam Onvoltooid Verleden*, Amsterdam, 1996

Liagre Böhl, H. de, *Amsterdam op de helling. De strijd om de stadsvernieuwing*, Amsterdam, 2010

Lörzing, H., *Van Bosplan tot Floriade*, Rotterdam, 1992

Luursema, E., & B. Mulder, *Handboek Renovatie Gordel 20-40 – Architectuurherstel in Amsterdam*, Bussum, 1995

Mattie, E. & J. Derwig, *Amsterdam School*, Amsterdam, 1991

Mattie, E. & J. Derwig, *Functionalism in the Netherlands*, Amsterdam, 1995

Meinsma, H. (ed.), *Schoonheid van Amsterdam, een kader voor het welstandsbeleid*, Amsterdam, 1994

Meischke, R., *Het Nederlandse Woonhuis van 1300-1800*, Haarlem, 1969

Moes, C.D.H., *Architectuurtekeningen uit het archief van J.D. Zocher jr. en L.P. Zocher*, Rotterdam, 1991

Molema, J., *Ir. J. Duiker*, Rotterdam, 1989
Nederlandse Architectuur 1910-1930, Amsterdamse School, ex.cat., Amsterdam, 1975

Neurderburg, E., *Hendrick de Keyser*,

Beeldhouwer en Bouwmeester van
Amsterdam, Amsterdam, z.j.
Nieuwe Bouwen Amsterdam 1920-1960,
ex.cat., Delft, 1983

Ottenheym, K., Philips Vingboons architect
1607-1678, Zutphen, 1989

Ottens, E., 125 jaar sociale woningbouw in
Amsterdam, Amsterdam, 1975

Ozinga, M.D., Daniël Marot, schepper van den
Hollandschen Lodewijk XIV stijl, Amsterdam
1938

Peet, C. van der & G. Steenmeijer (ed.),
De Rijksbouwmeesters, Rotterdam, 1995

Pistor, R. (ed.), A City in Progress: physical
planning in Amsterdam, Amsterdam, 1994

Polano, S., et al., H.P. Berlage Complete
Works, New York, 1988

Rebel, B., et al., Ben Merkelbach. Architect en
Stadsbouwmeester, Amsterdam, 1994

Reinink, A.W., Herman Hertzberger Architect,
Rotterdam, 1991

Révész-Alexander, M., Die alten Lagerhäuser
Amsterdams, ein kunstgeschichtliche
Studie, 's-Gravenhage, 1928

Roegholt, R., Amsterdam na 1900,
's-Gravenhage, 1993

Rosenberg, H.P.R., De negentiende-eeuwse
kerkelijke bouwkunst in Nederland,
's-Gravenhage, 1993

Rossem, V. van, Het Algemeen Uitbreidingsplan
van Amsterdam: geschiedenis en ontwerp,
Rotterdam, 1993

Rossem, V. van (ed.), Amsterdam maakt
geschiedenis, Amsterdam, 2004

Roy van Zuydewijn, H.J.F. de, Amsterdamse
Bouwkunst 1815-1940, Amsterdam, 1970

Schade, C., Woningbouw voor arbeiders in het
negentiende-eeuwse Amsterdam,
Amsterdam, 1970

Schilt, J. & J. van der Werf, Genootschap
Architectura et Amicitia 1855-1990,
Rotterdam, 1992

Singelenberg, P., H.P. Berlage, Idea and Style,
Utrecht, 1972

Slothouwer, D.F., Amsterdamse Huizen
1600-1800, Amsterdam, 1928

Smit, F.V., Bruggen in Amsterdam. Infrastructu-
rele ontwikkelingen en brugontwerpen van

1850 tot 2010, Utrecht, 2010

Spies, P. (ed.), et al., Canals of Amsterdam,
's-Gravenhage, 1991

Spies, P,. et al., Grachtenboek II, middel-
eeuwsestadskern, 's-Gravenhage, 1992

Stieber, N., Housing design and society in
Amsterdam. Reconfiguring Urban Order and
Identity, 1900-1920, Chicago & London,
1998

Strauven, F., Aldo van Eyck, relativity and
imagination, Amsterdam, 1996

Swigchem, C.A. van, Abraham van der Hart
1747-1820, Architect en Stadsbouw meester
van Amsterdam, Amsterdam, 1965

Taverne, E., In 't land van belofte: in de nieuwe
stadt, Maarssen, 1978

Valk, A. v.d., Amsterdam in aanleg, Amsterdam,
1989

Vermeulen, F.A.J., Handboek tot de Geschiedenis
der Nederlandsche Bouwkunst, 's-Gravenhage,
1928

Vreeken, B. & E. Wouthuysen, Grand Hotels van
Amsterdam. opkomst en bloei sinds 1860,
's-Gravenhage, 1987

Vroom, W., et al., Vincenzo Scamozzi Venetian
Architect. The Idea of a Universal Architecture
Book III Villas and Country Estates,
Amsterdam, 2003

Vroom, W., et al., Vincenzo Scamozzi Venetian
Architect. The Architectural Orders and their
Application Book VI, Amsterdam, 2008

Wallagh, G., Oog voor het onzichtbare, 50 jaar
structuurplanning in Amsterdam 1855-2005,
Assen, 1994

Wattjes, J.G. & F.A. Warners, Amsterdamse
Bouwkunst en Stadsschoon, Amsterdam,
1944

Wit, W. de, The Amsterdam School, Dutch
Expressionist Architecture 1915-1930,
Cambridge, 1984

Wijnman, H.F., Historische Gids van Amsterdam.
revised edition. Amsterdam, 1971

Wijnman, H.F., Vier eeuwen Herengracht,
Amsterdam, 1974

Zantkuyl, H.J., Bouwen in Amsterdam,
Amsterdam, 2007

Zantkuyl, H.J., et al., Huizen in Nederland:
Amsterdam, Zwolle, 1995

Index

Figures in **bold** correspond with the bold numbered captions of the images.

262

Photo credits

Adresses

The following institutions are engaged in research and/or training in the field of architecture or are addresses for information on architectural activities.

Academy of Architecture, Waterlooplein 211, 1011 PG Amsterdam,
www.academievanbouwkunst.nl
Amsterdam City Archives, Vijzelstraat 32, 1017 HL Amsterdam,
www.stadsarchief.amsterdam.nl
Amsterdam Historical Museum, Nieuwezijds Voorburgwal 359,
1012 RM Amsterdam, www.ahm.nl
Amsterdamse School Museum Het Schip, Spaarndammerplantsoen 140,
1013 XT Amsterdam, www.hetschip.nl
ARCAM Architectuurcentrum Amsterdam, Prins Hendrikkade 600,
1011 VX Amsterdam, www.arcam.nl
Architectura & Natura Booksellers, Leliegracht 22, 1015 DG Amsterdam,
www.architectura.nl
Beurs van Berlage, Damrak 277, 1012 LZ Amsterdam, www.beursvanberlage.nl
Bureau Monumenten & Archeologie, Herengracht 482, 1017 CB Amsterdam,
www.bma.amsterdam.nl
Gerrit Rietveld Academie, Fred Roeskestraat 96, 1076 ED Amsterdam,
www.gerritrietveldacademie.nl
Netherlands Architecture Institute (NAi), Museumpark 25, 3015 CB Rotterdam,
www.nai.nl
Rijksdienst voor het Cultureel Erfgoed, Smallepad 5, 3811 MG Amersfoort,
www.cultureelerfgoed.nl
Royal Institute of Dutch Architects (BNA), Jollemanhof 14, 1019 GW Amsterdam,
www.bna.nl
SKOR Stichting Kunst in de Openbare Ruimte, Ruysdaelkade 2,
1072 AG Amsterdam, www.skor.nl
Stichting Archivisie, Touwslagerstraat 13, 1013 DL Amsterdam,
www.monumenten.nl
University of Delft, Faculty of Architecture, Julianalaan 132-134, 2628 BL Delft,
www.bk.tudelft.nl
Vereniging Vrienden van de Amsterdamse Binnenstad, Sloterkade 21,
1058 HE Amsterdam, www.amsterdamsebinnenstad.nl

Dates

National day of architecture, organised by the BNA (Architectural Association)
– 1 July or last Sunday of June
National Monument Day, organised by Monumentenzorg (Municipal Monument
Care) – second Saterday of September